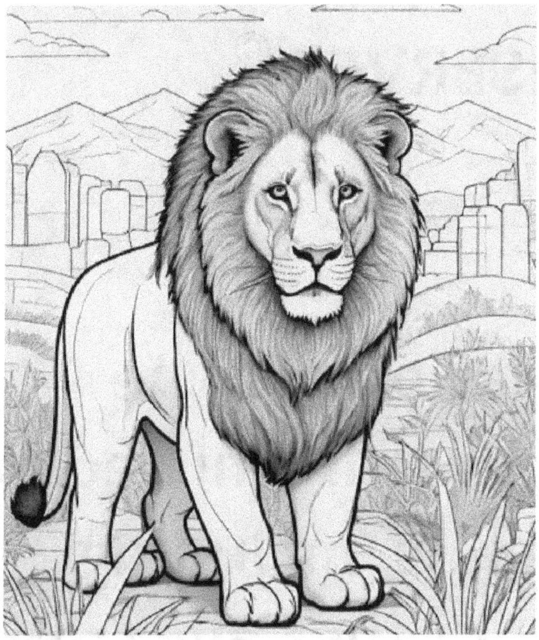

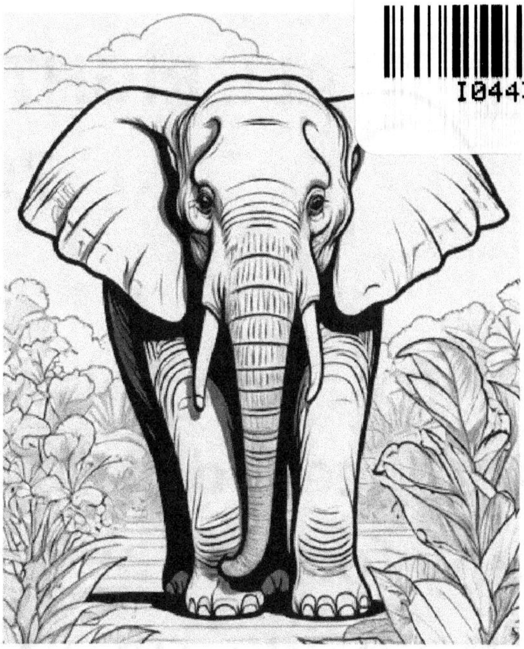

This Book Belongs to:

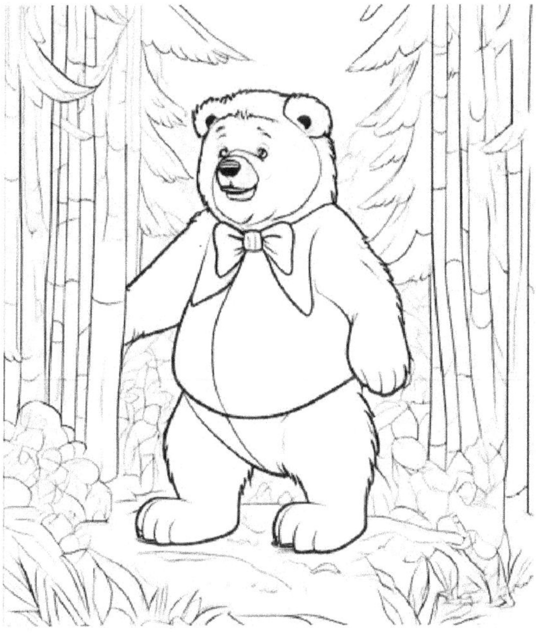

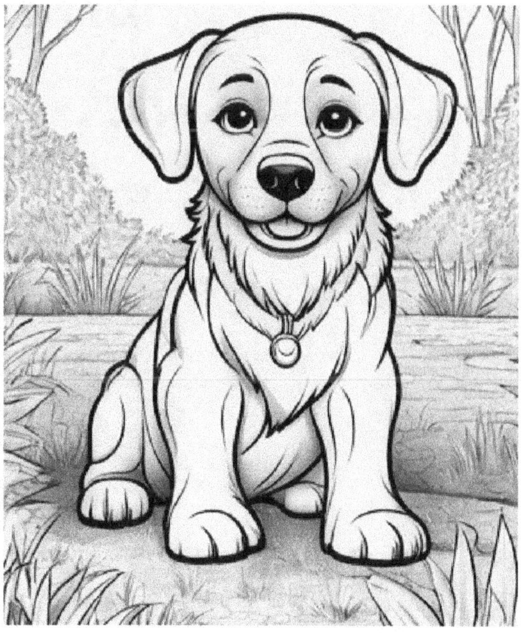

D.G.M.©
Denilso Gomes; publications

Test Color Page

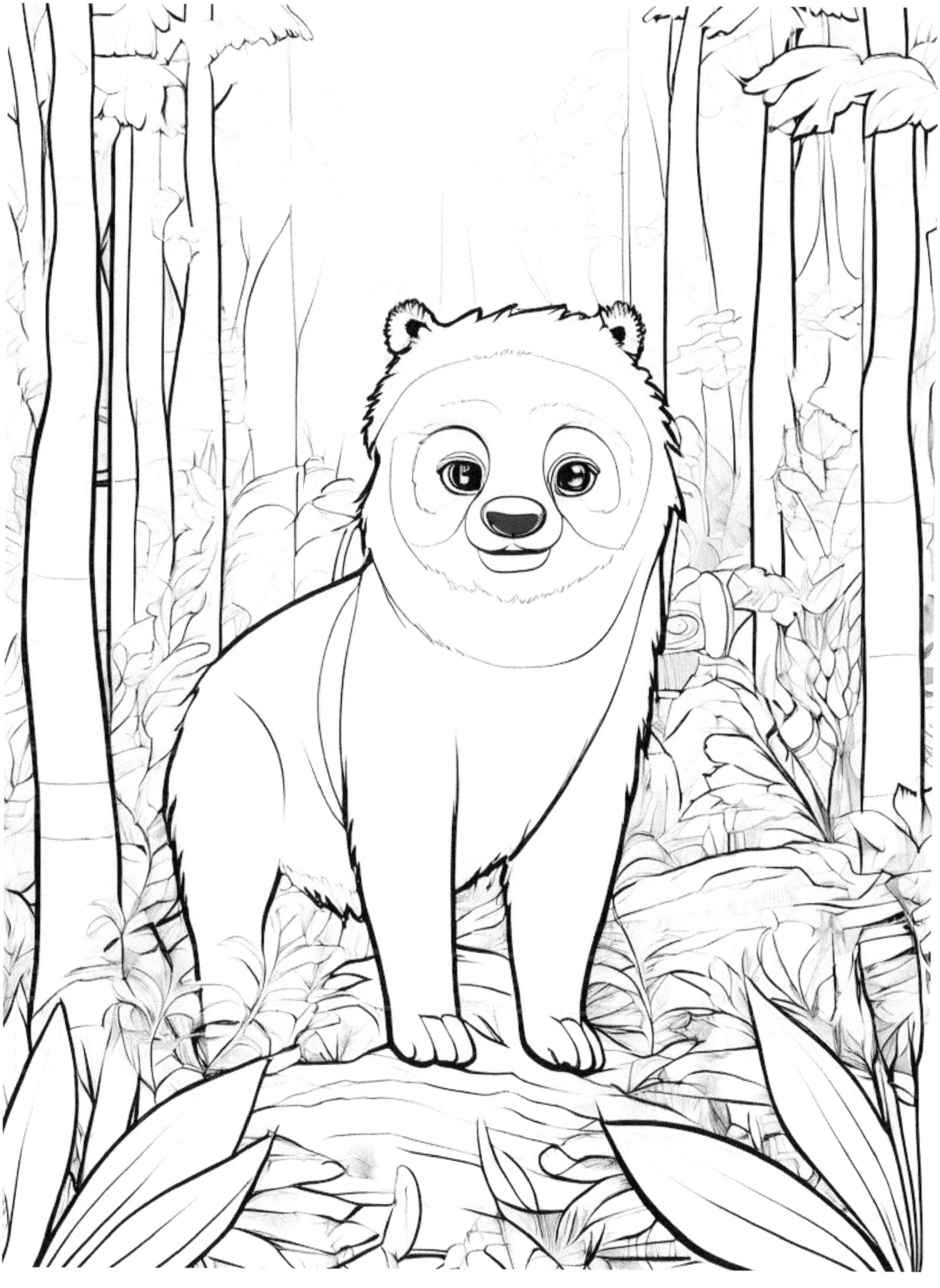

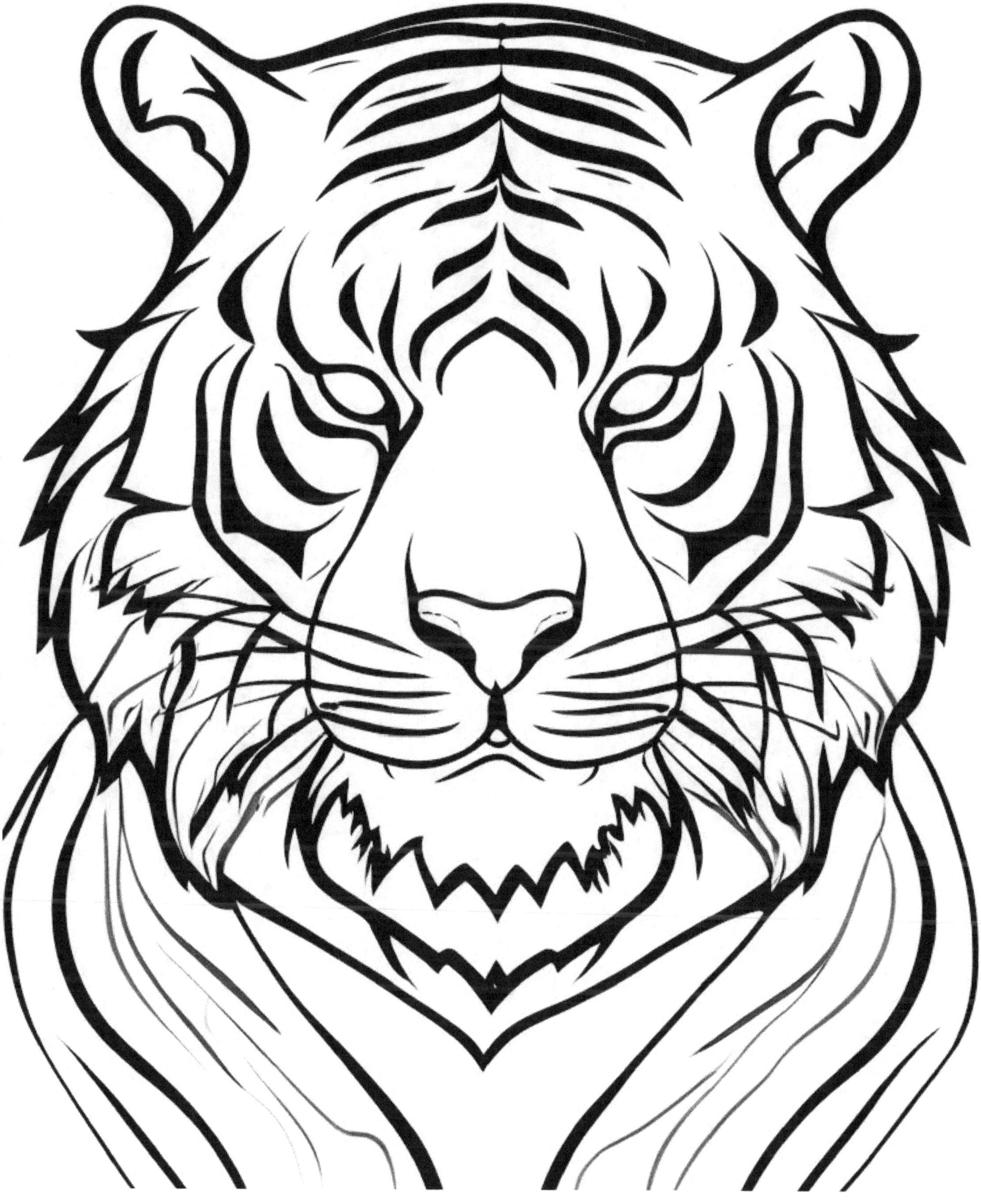

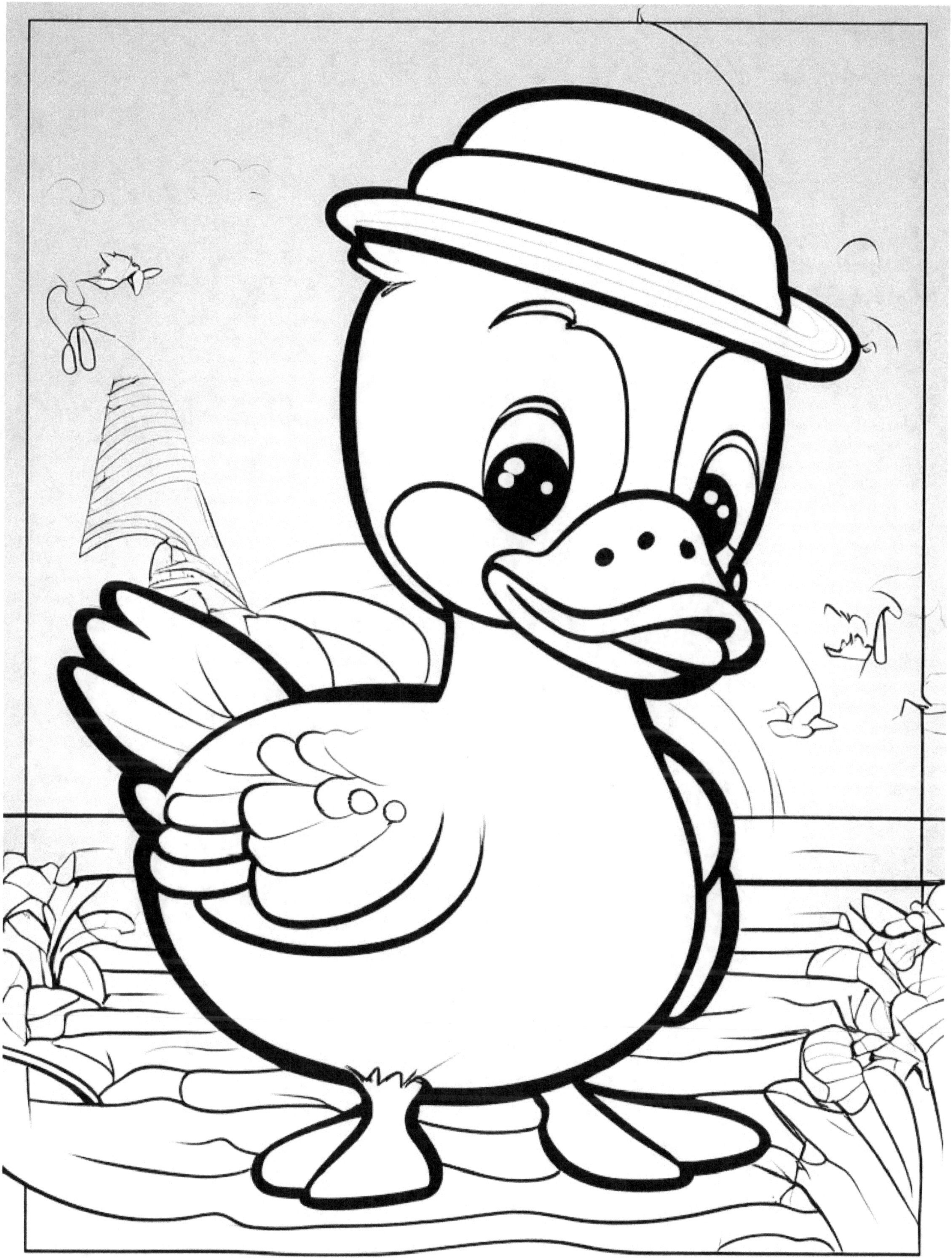

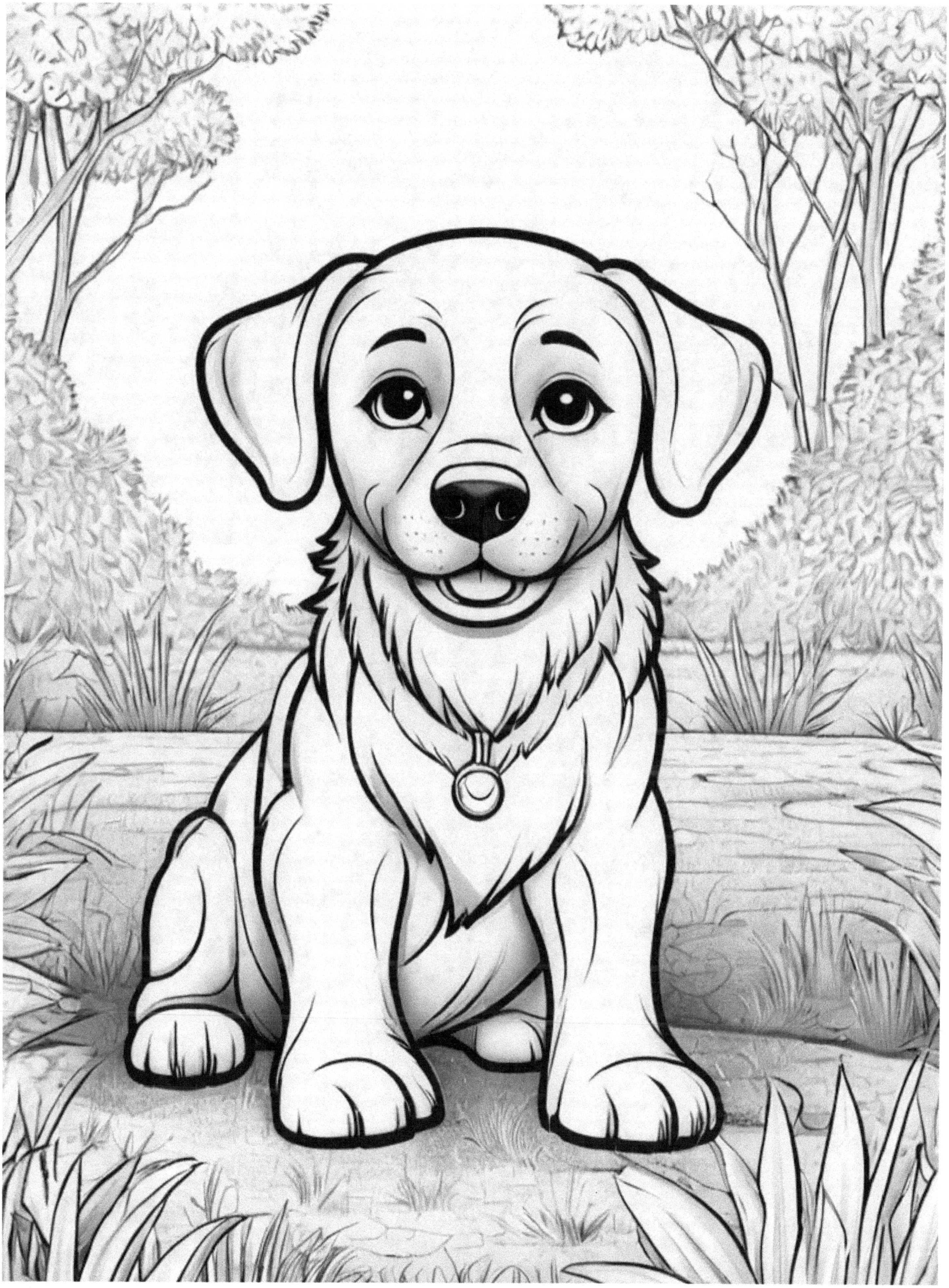

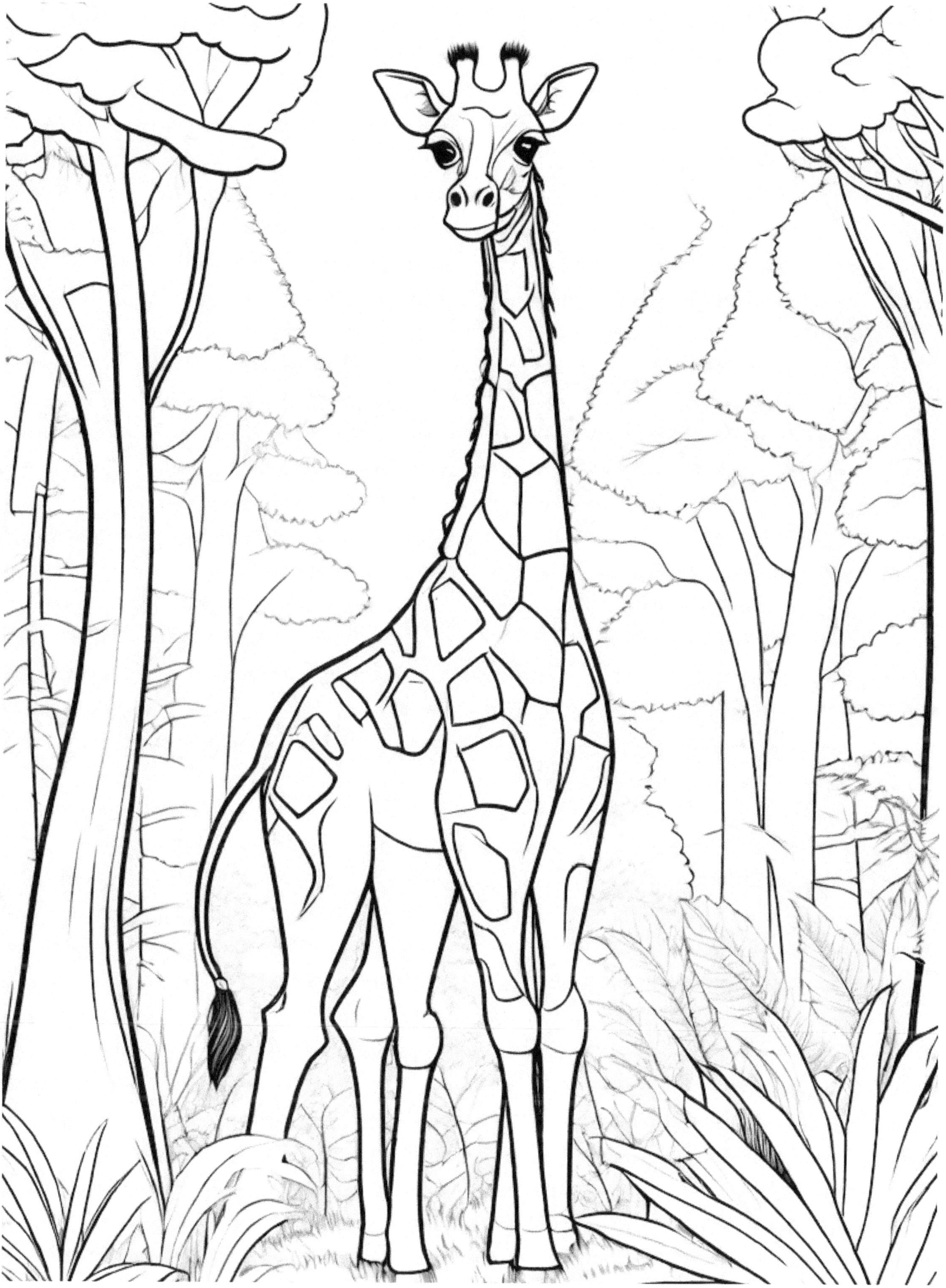

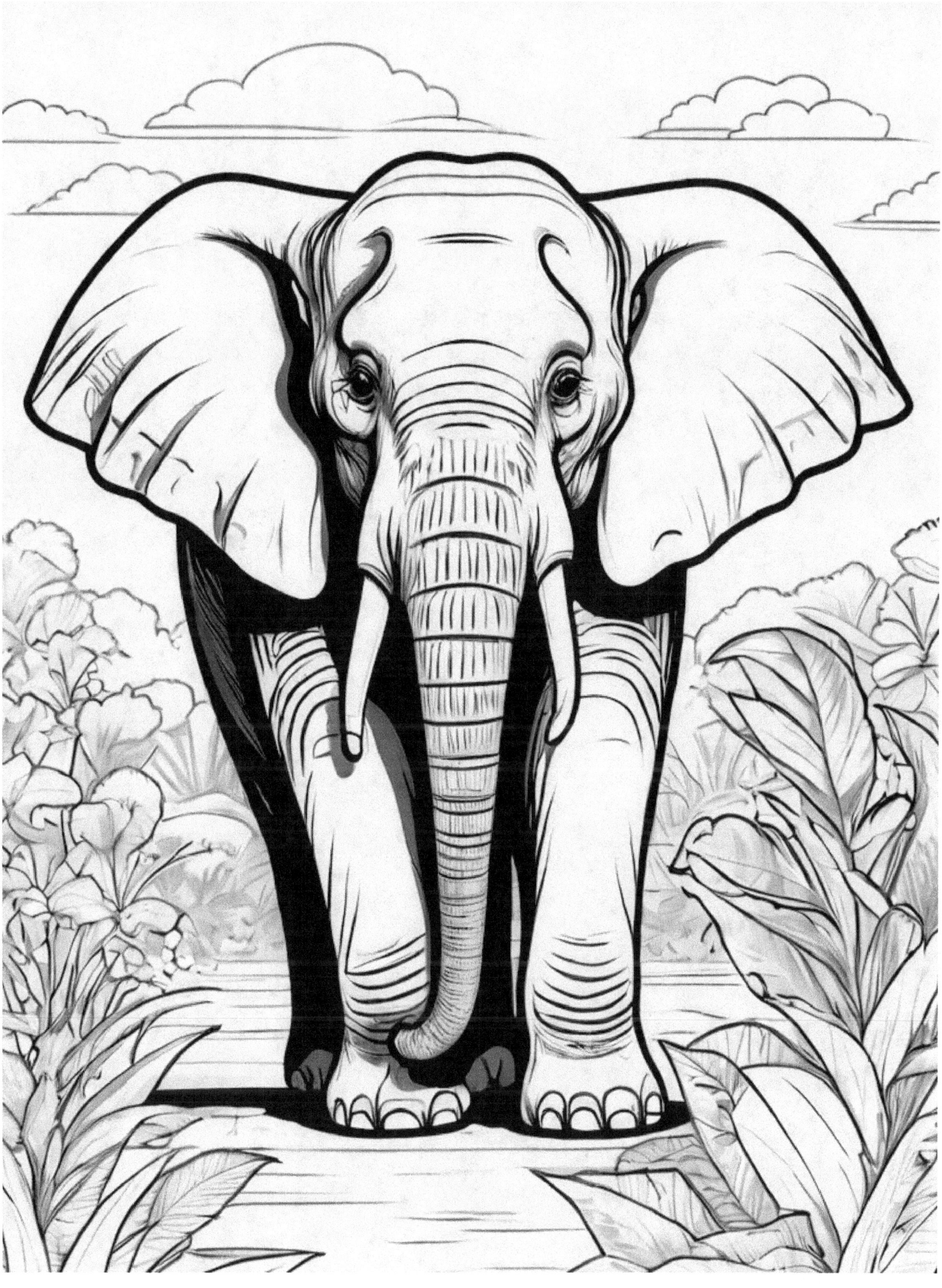

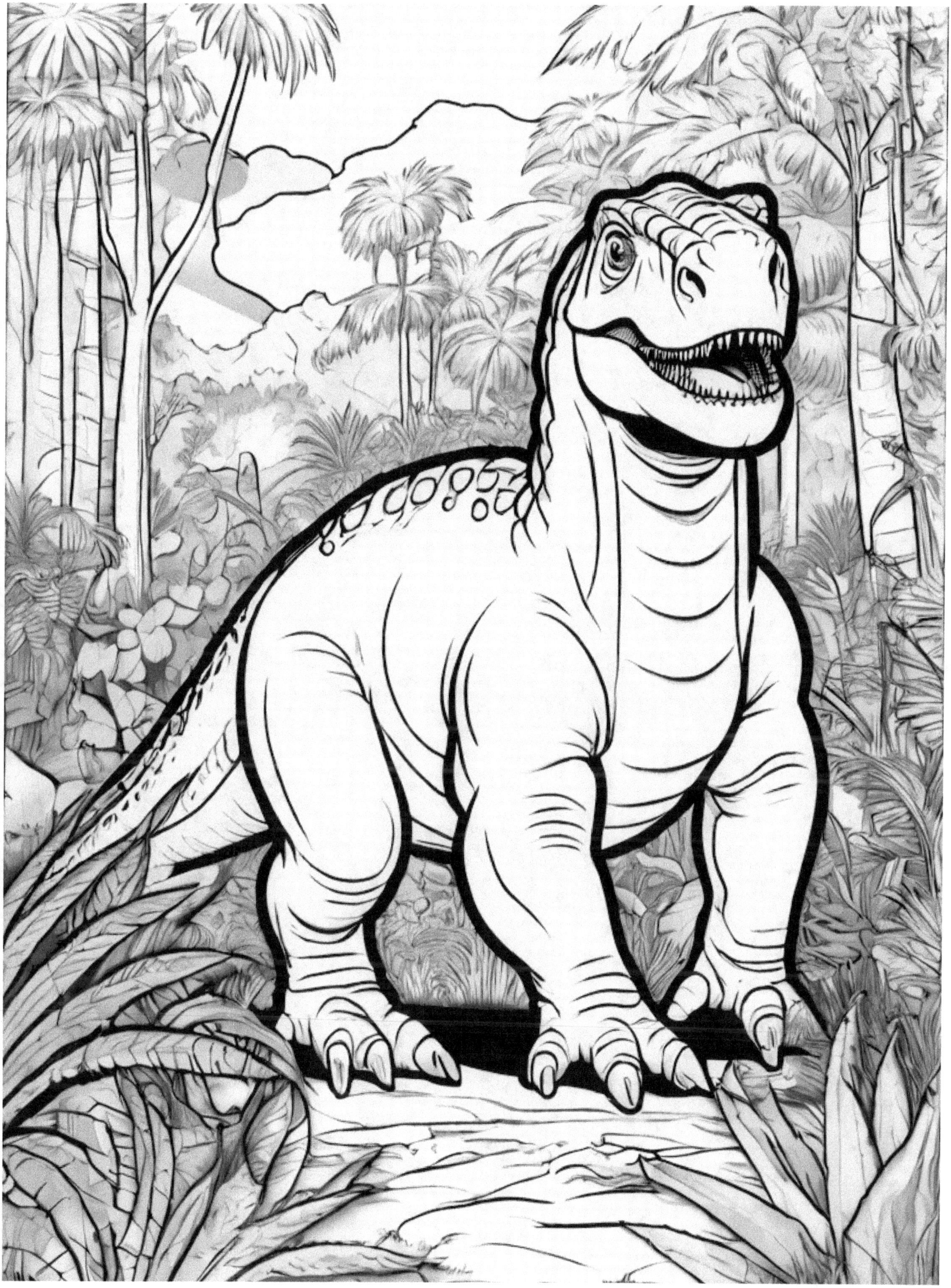

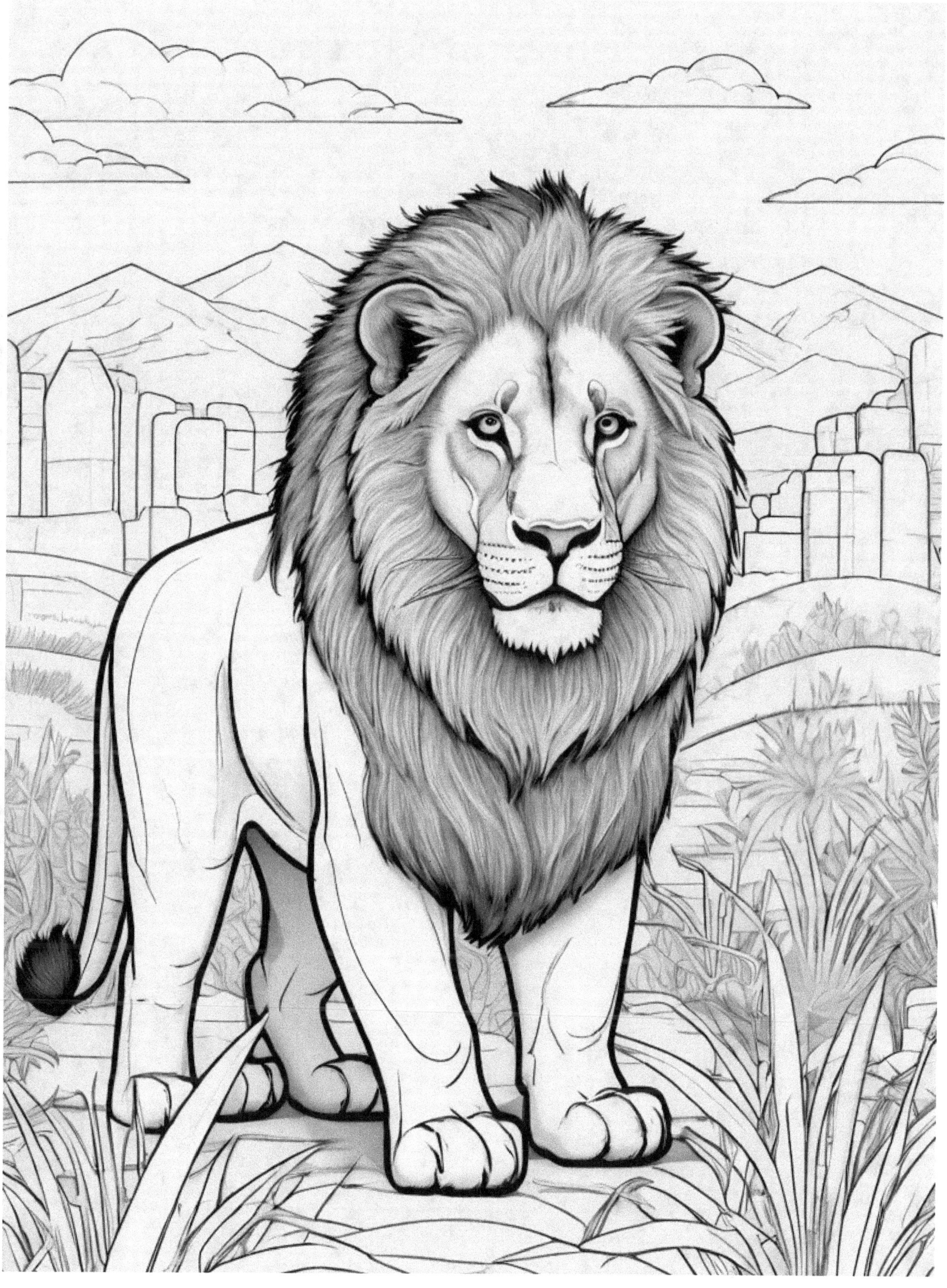

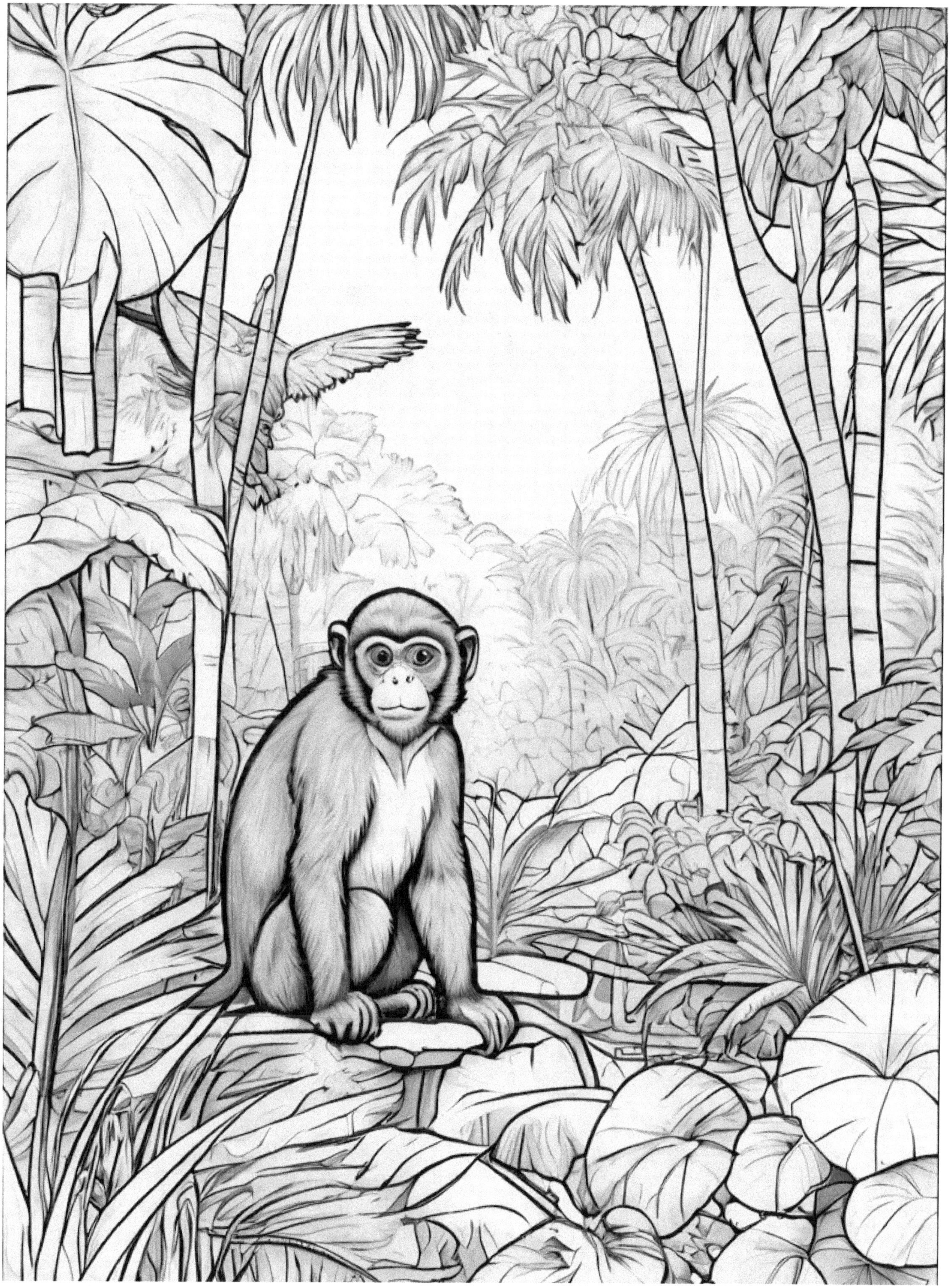

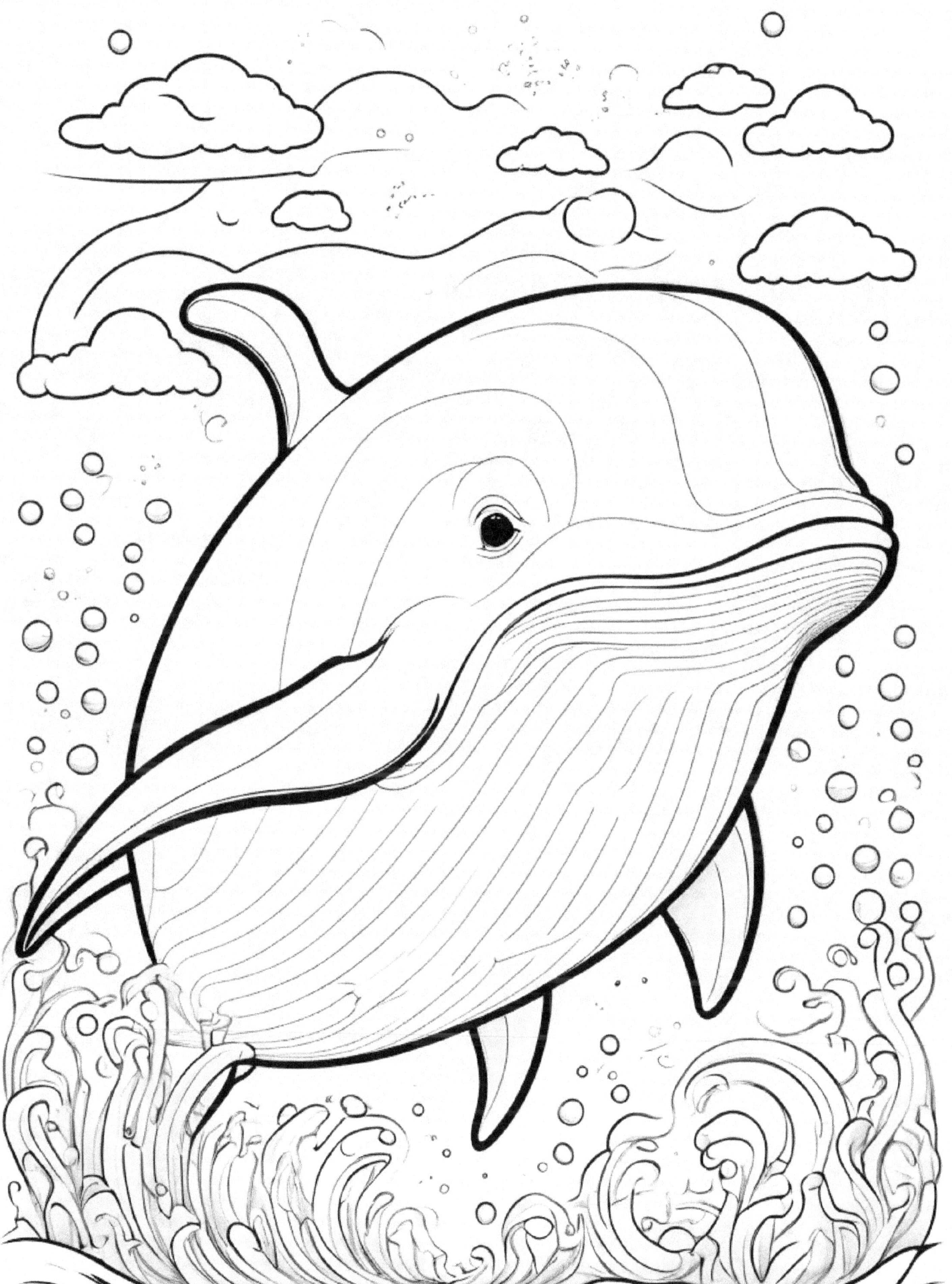

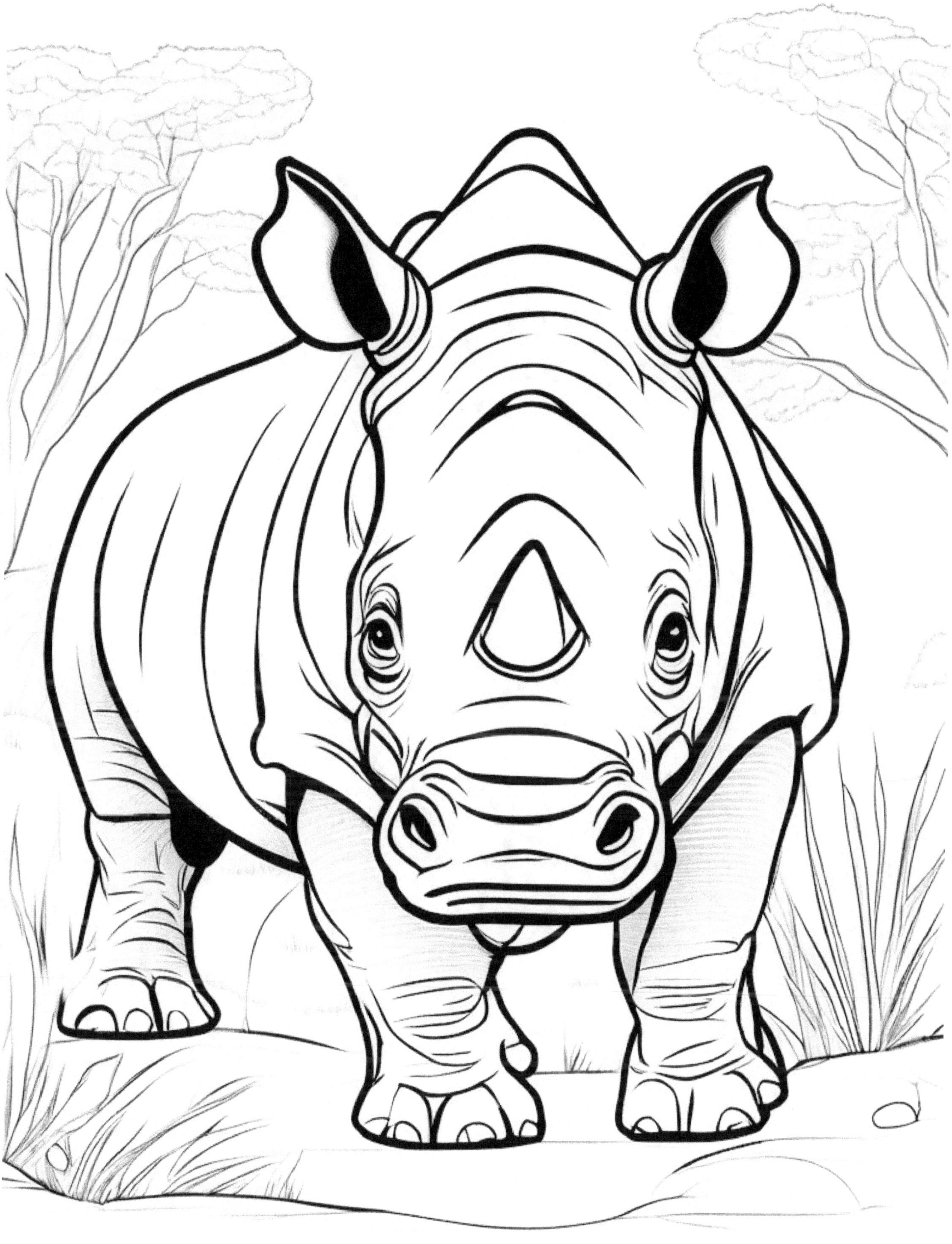

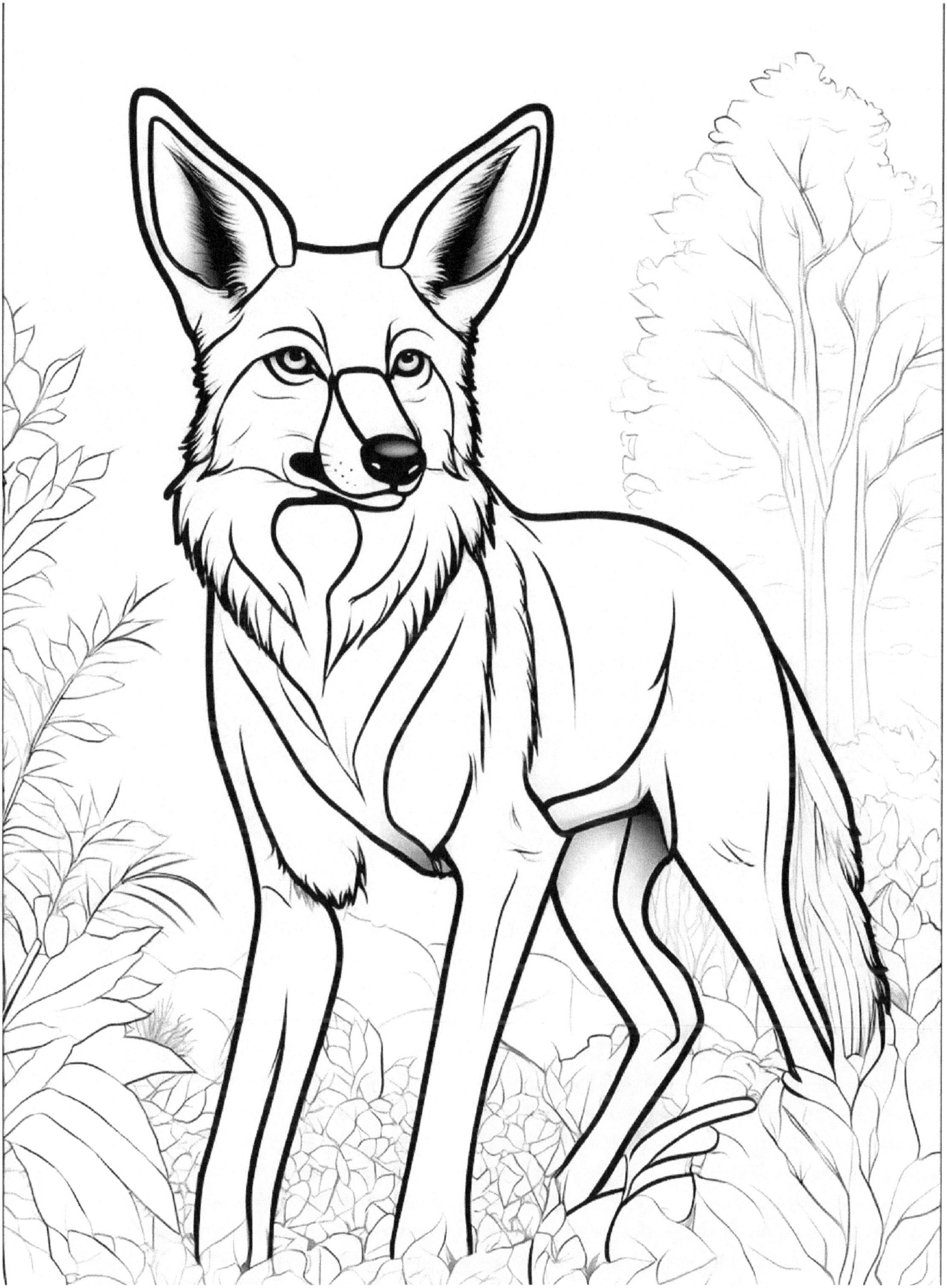

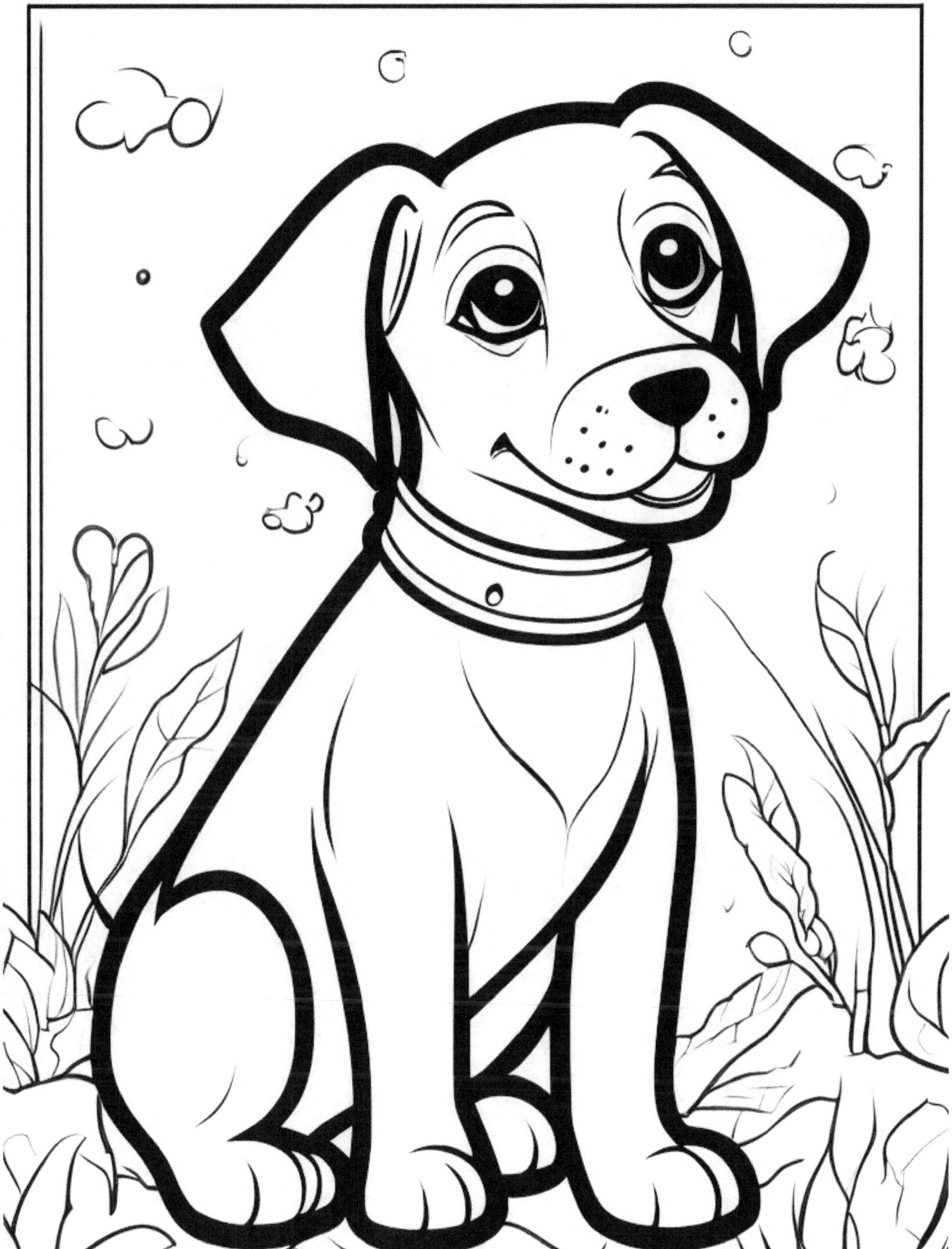

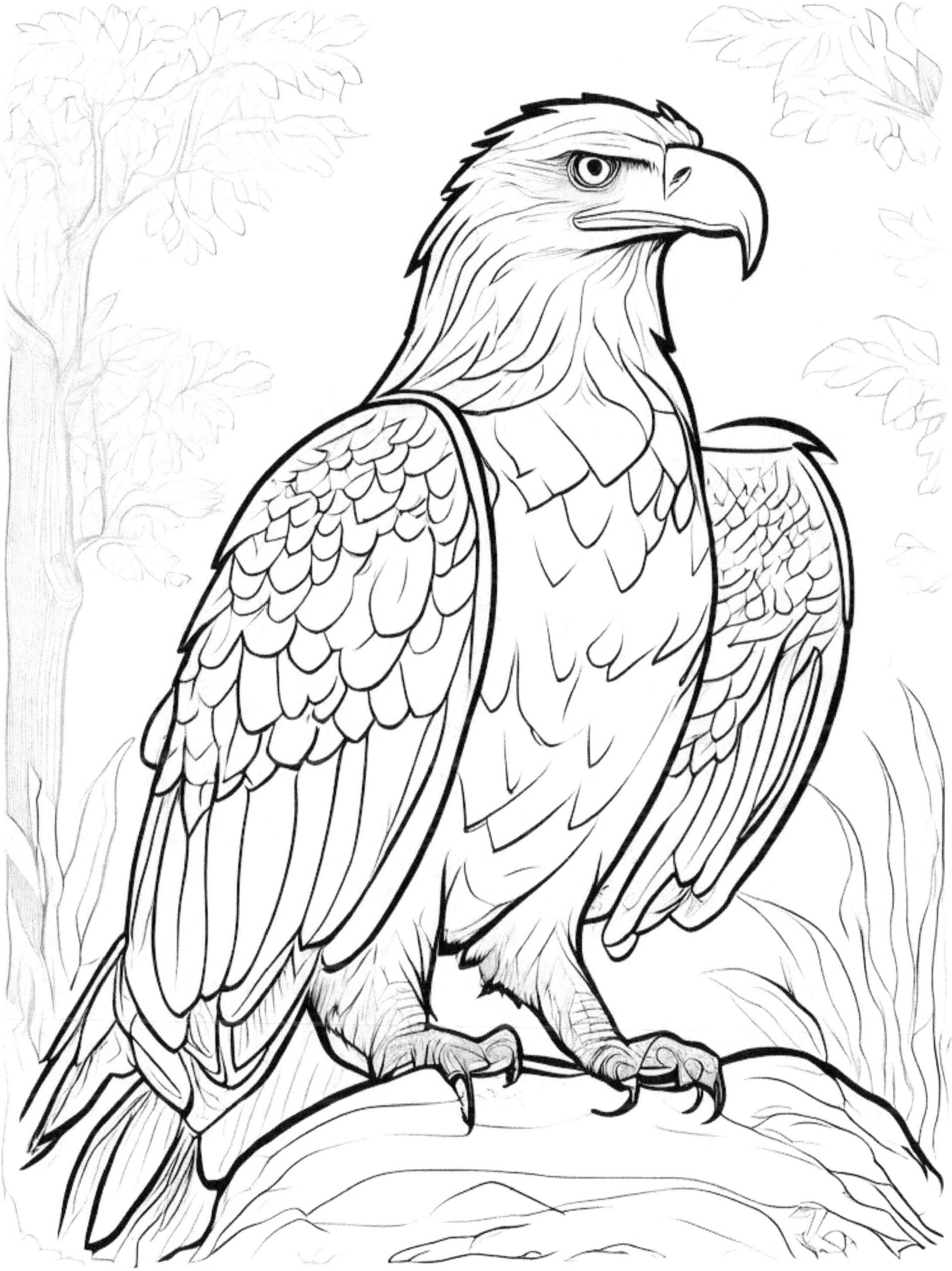

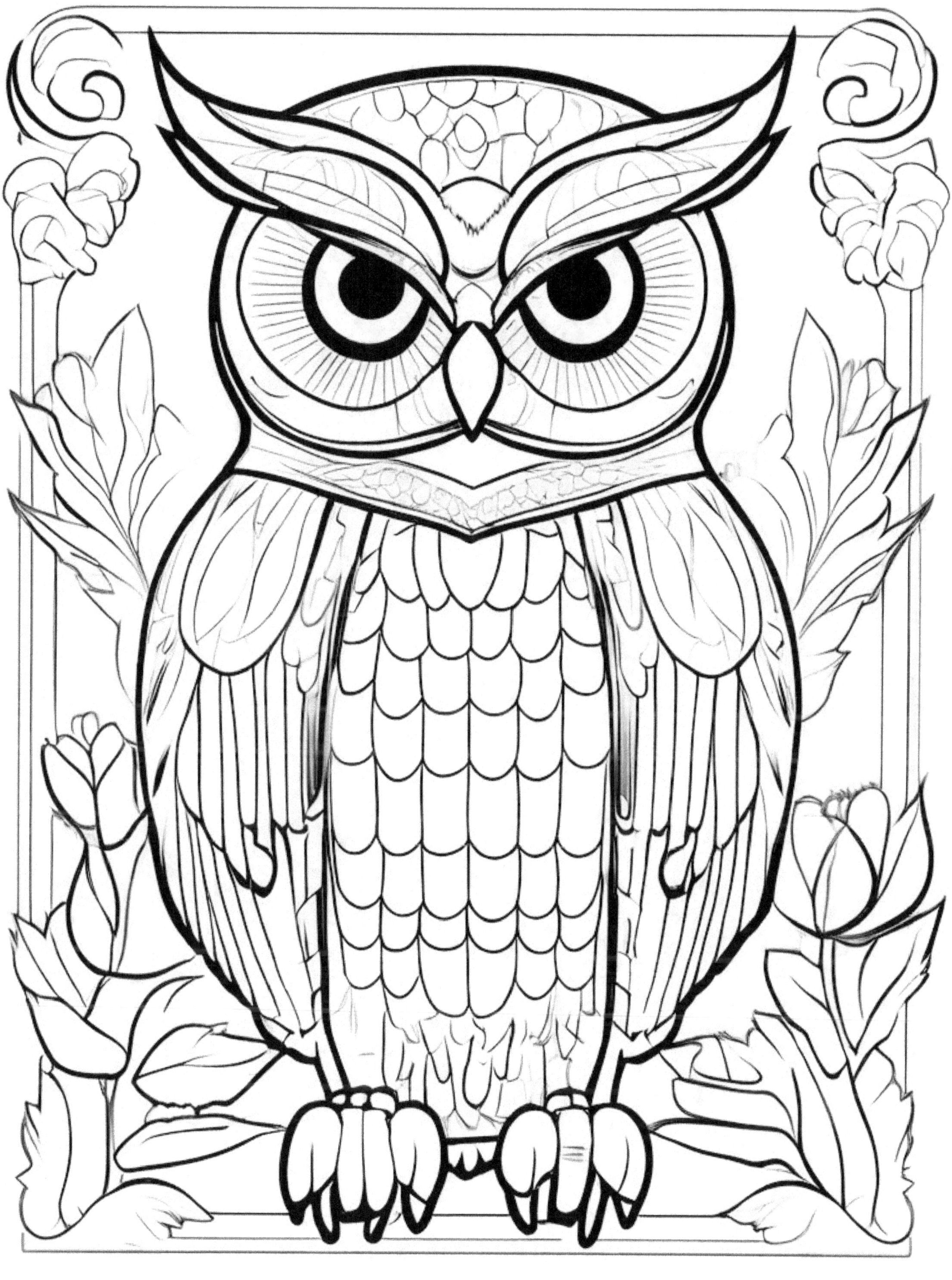

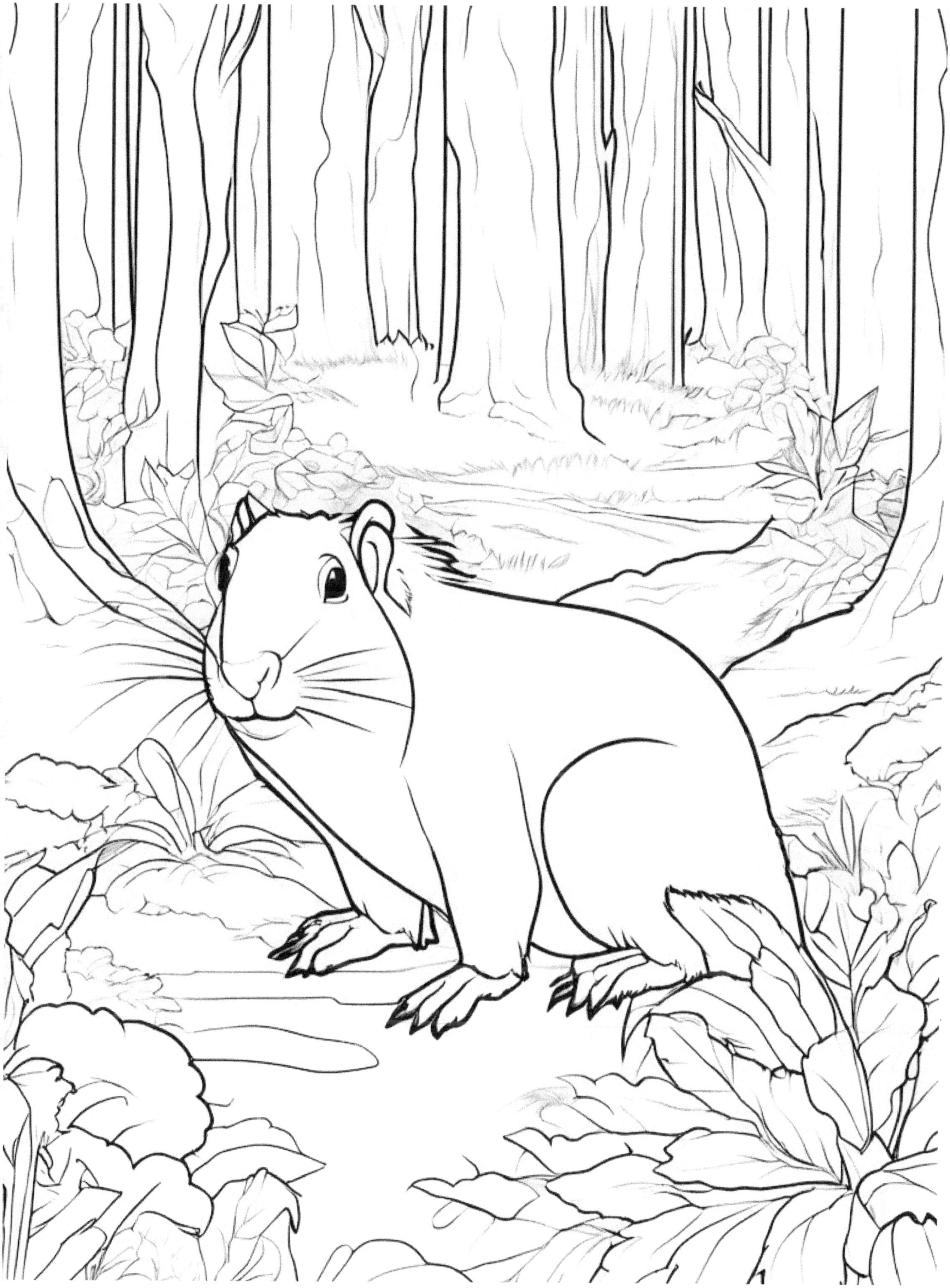

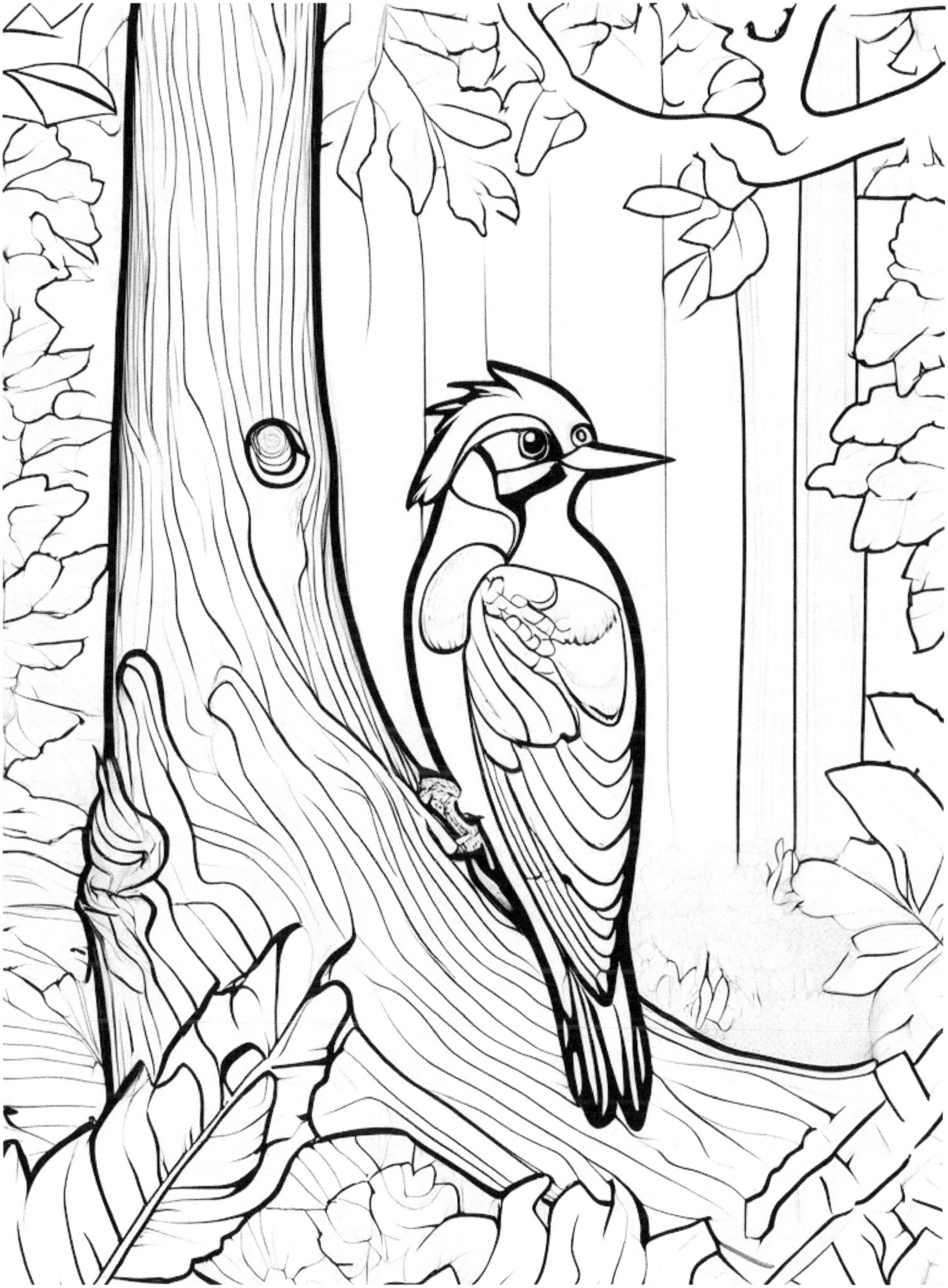

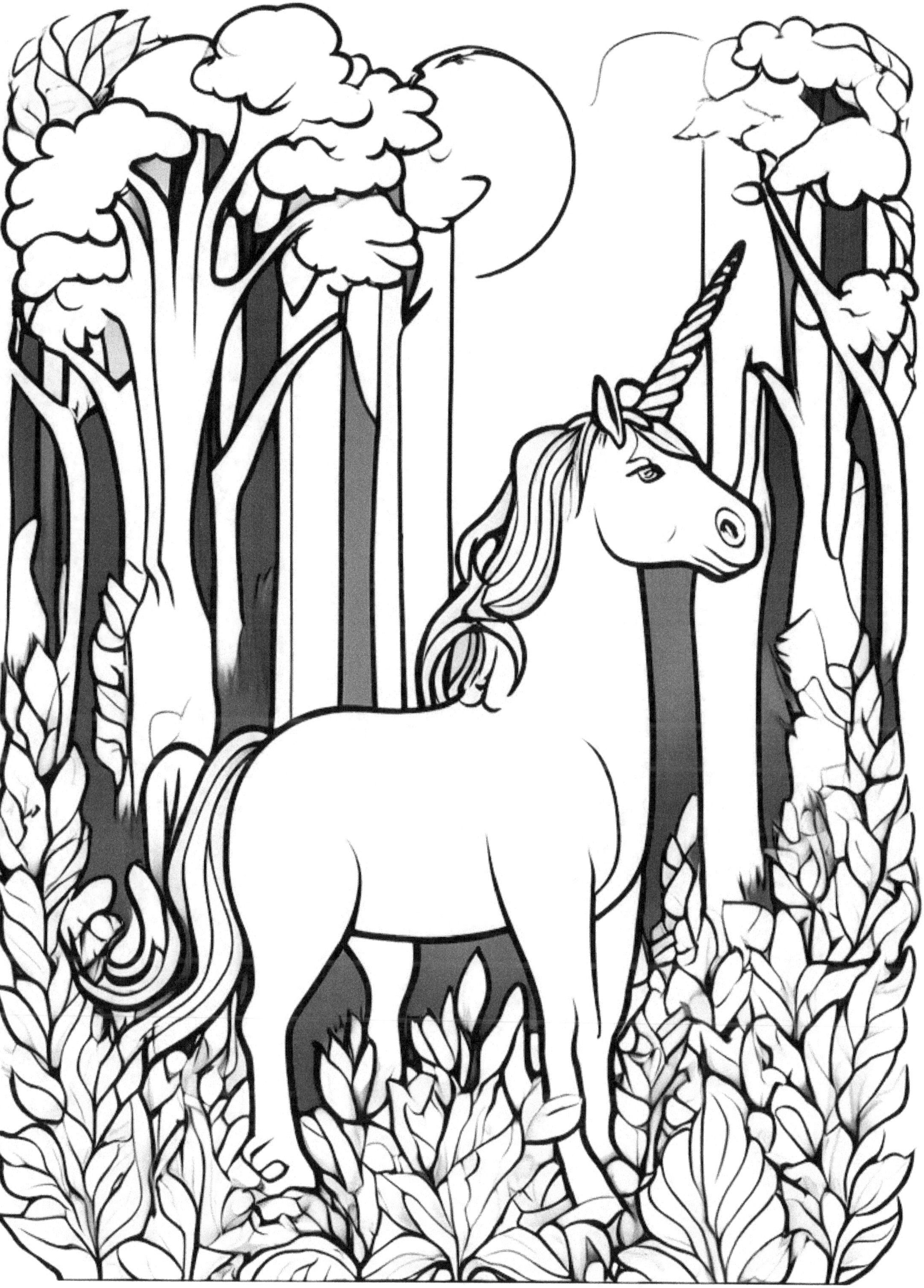

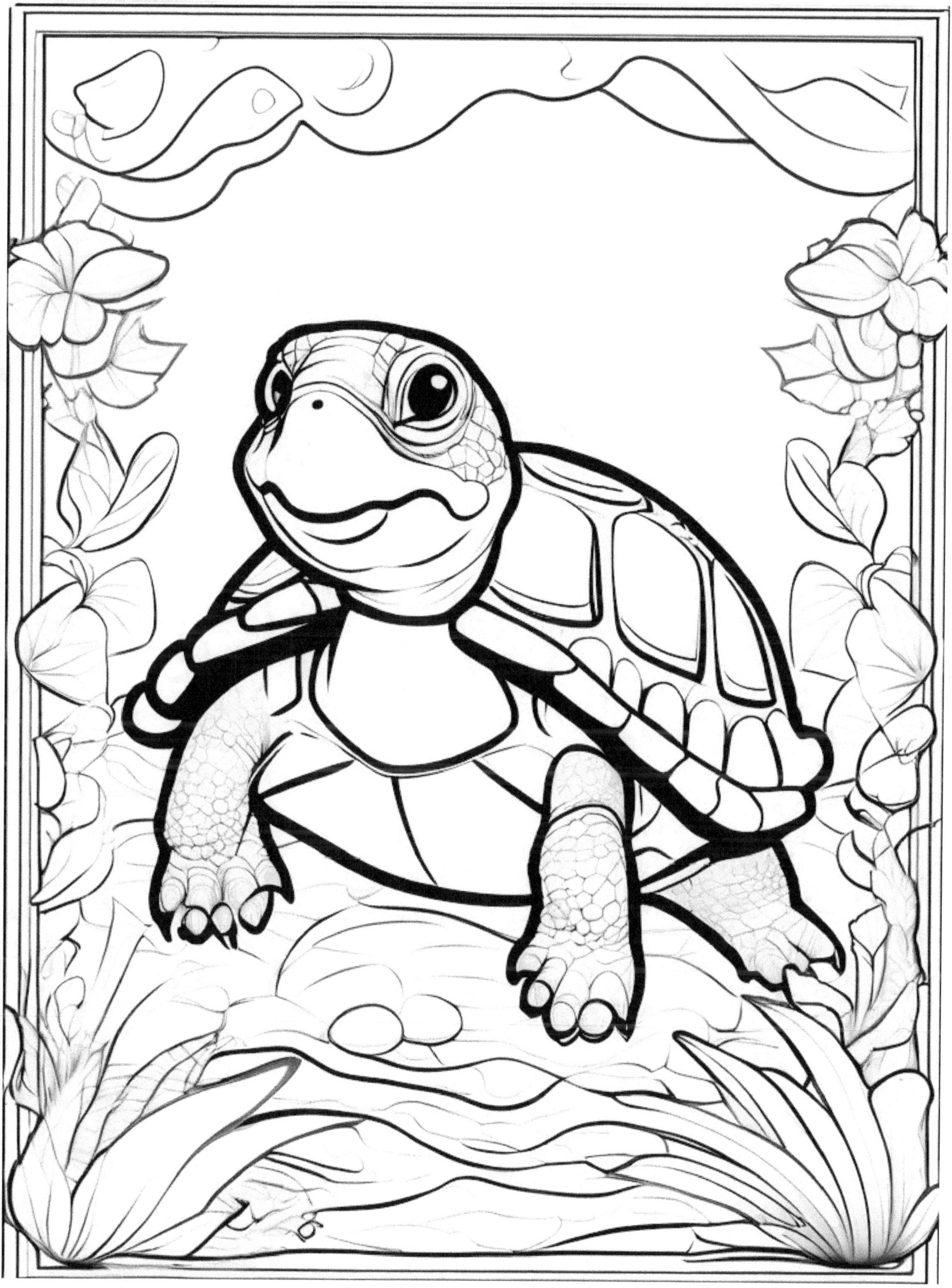

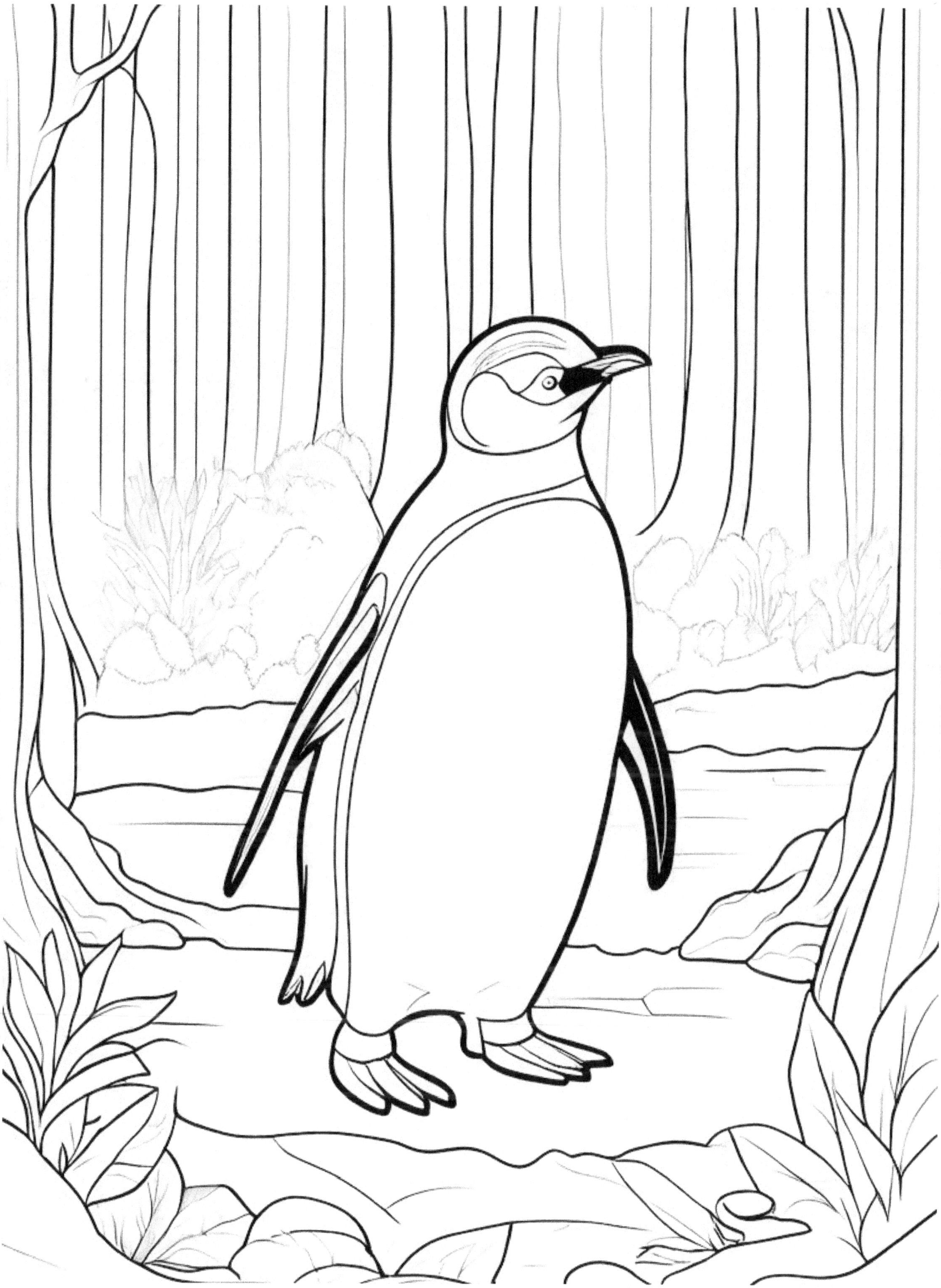

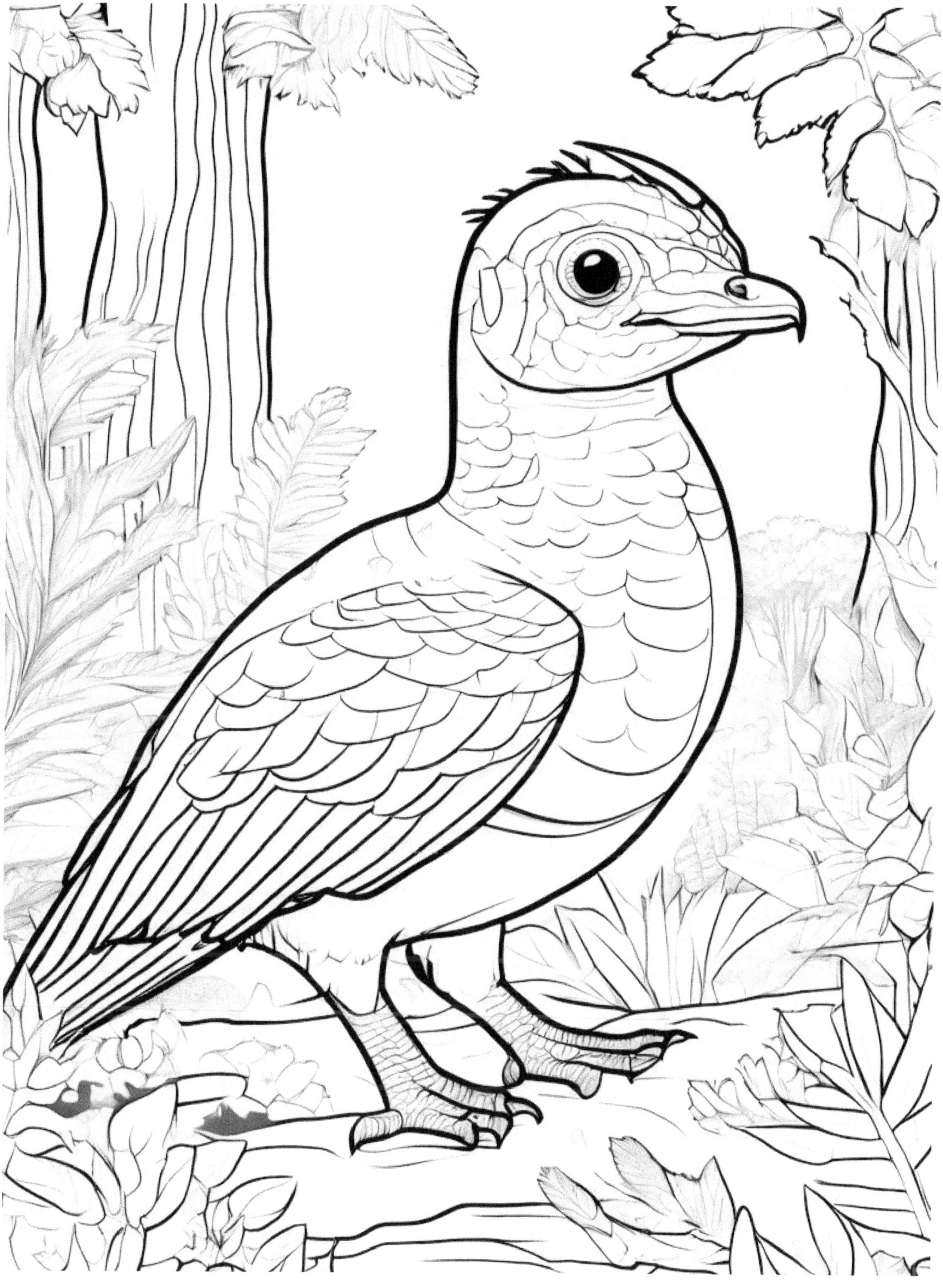

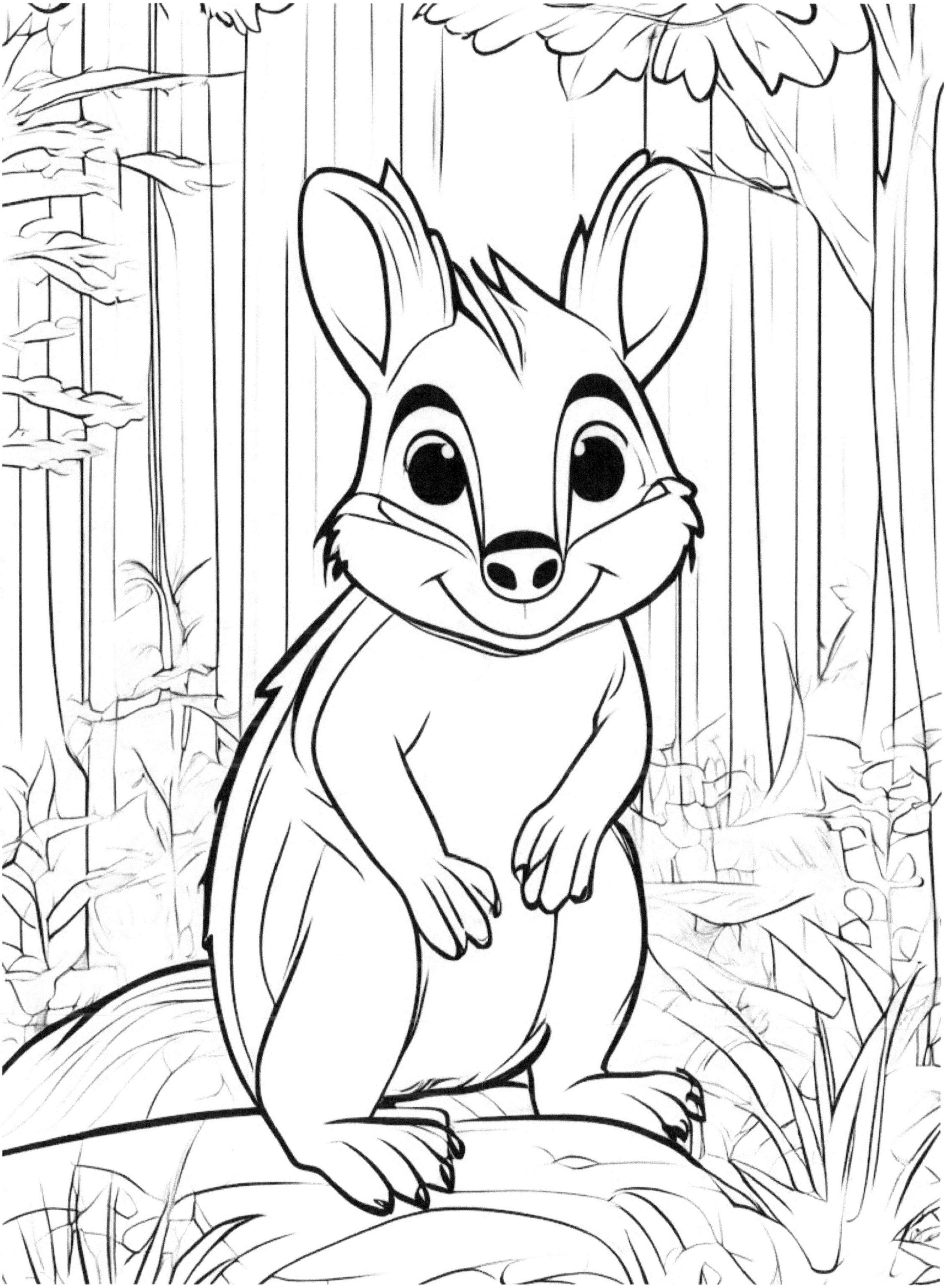

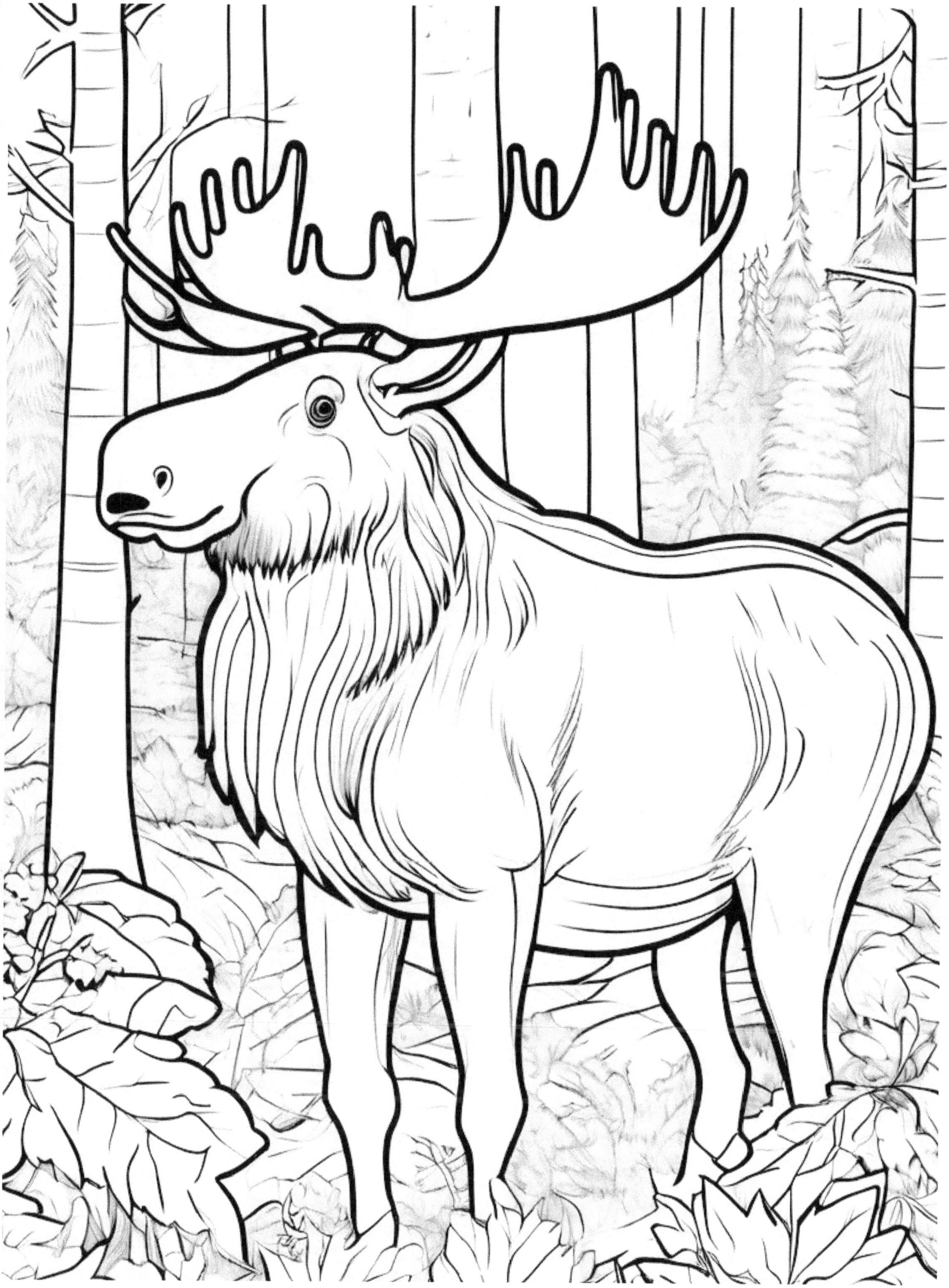

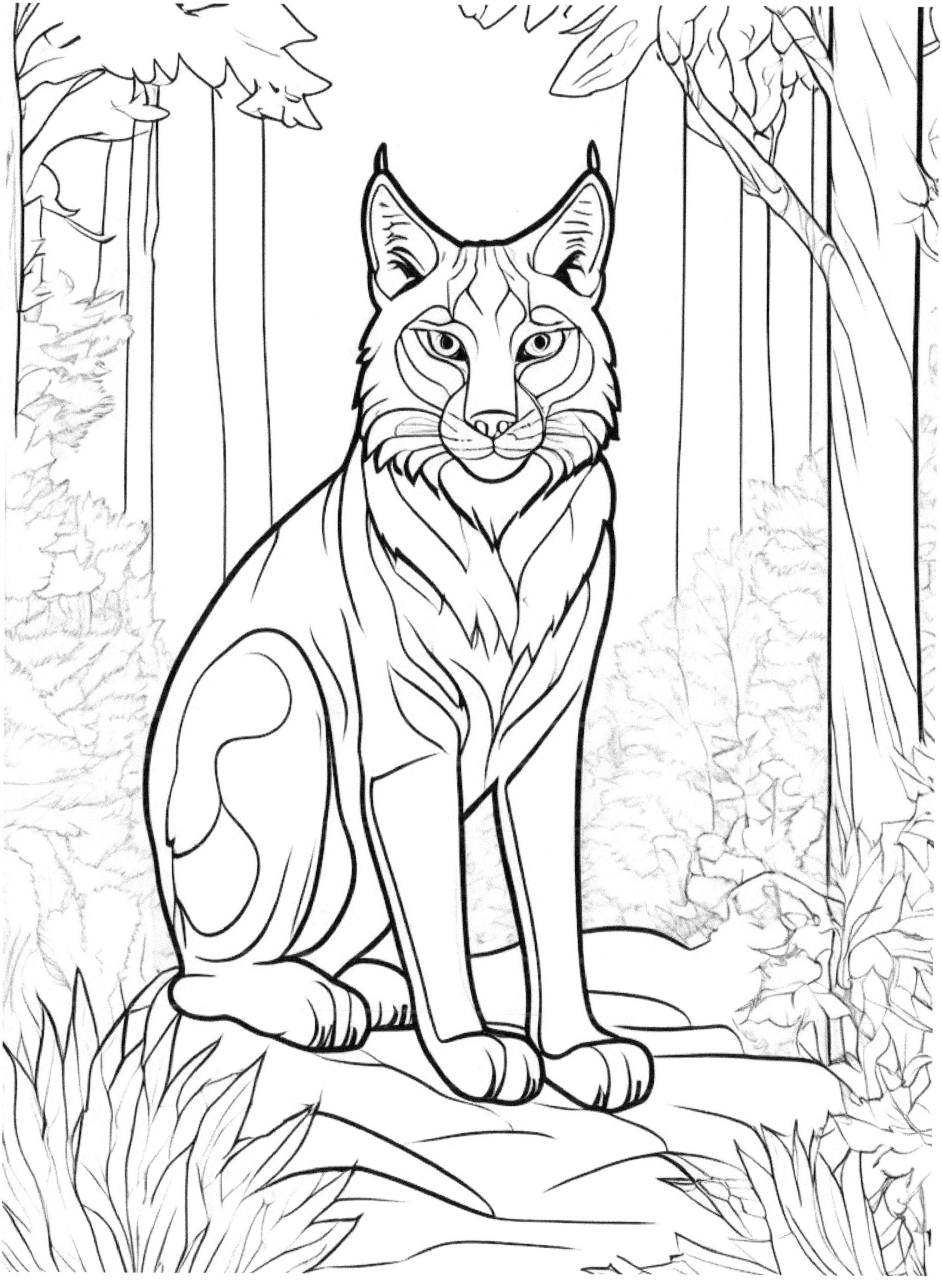

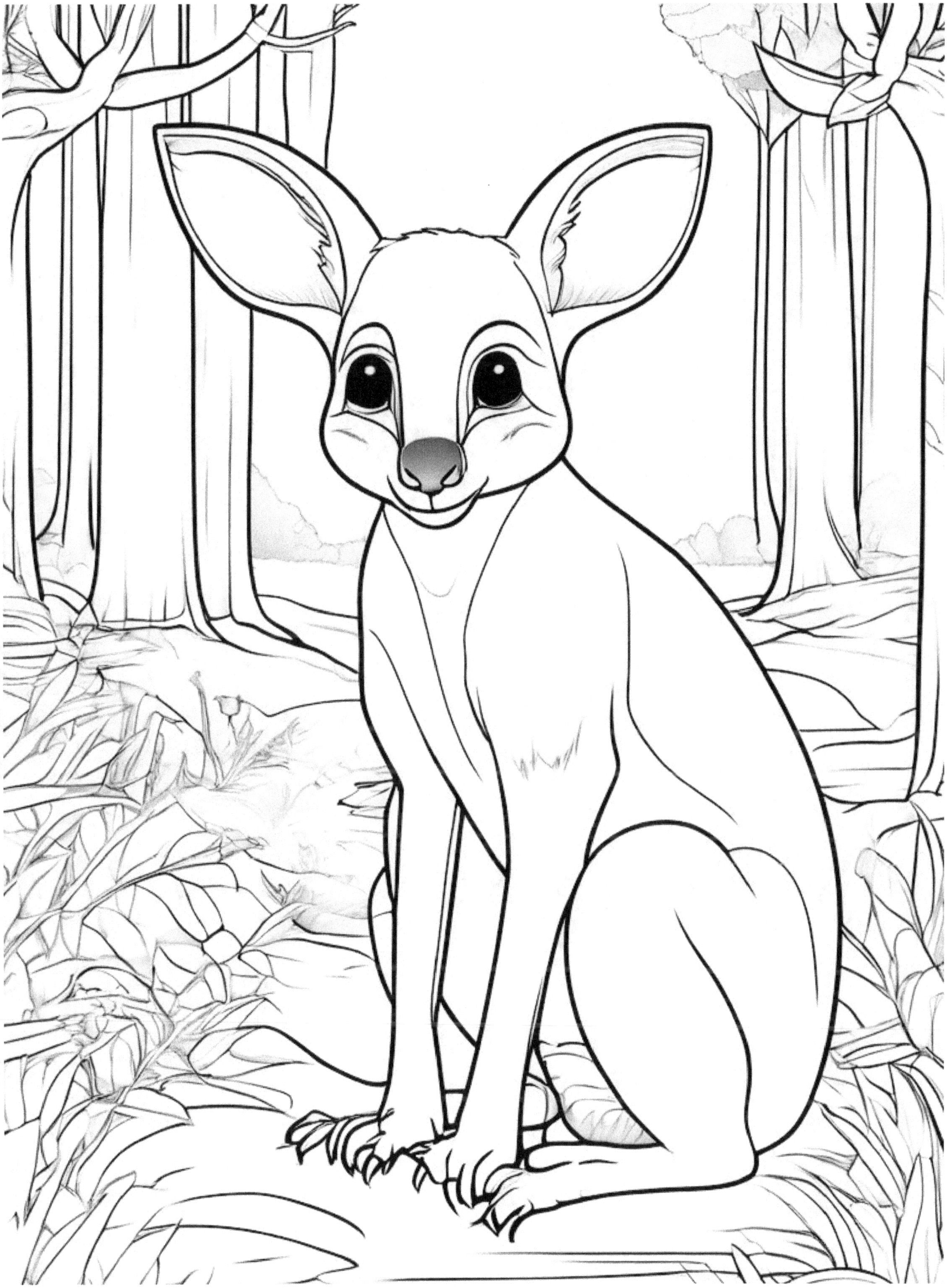

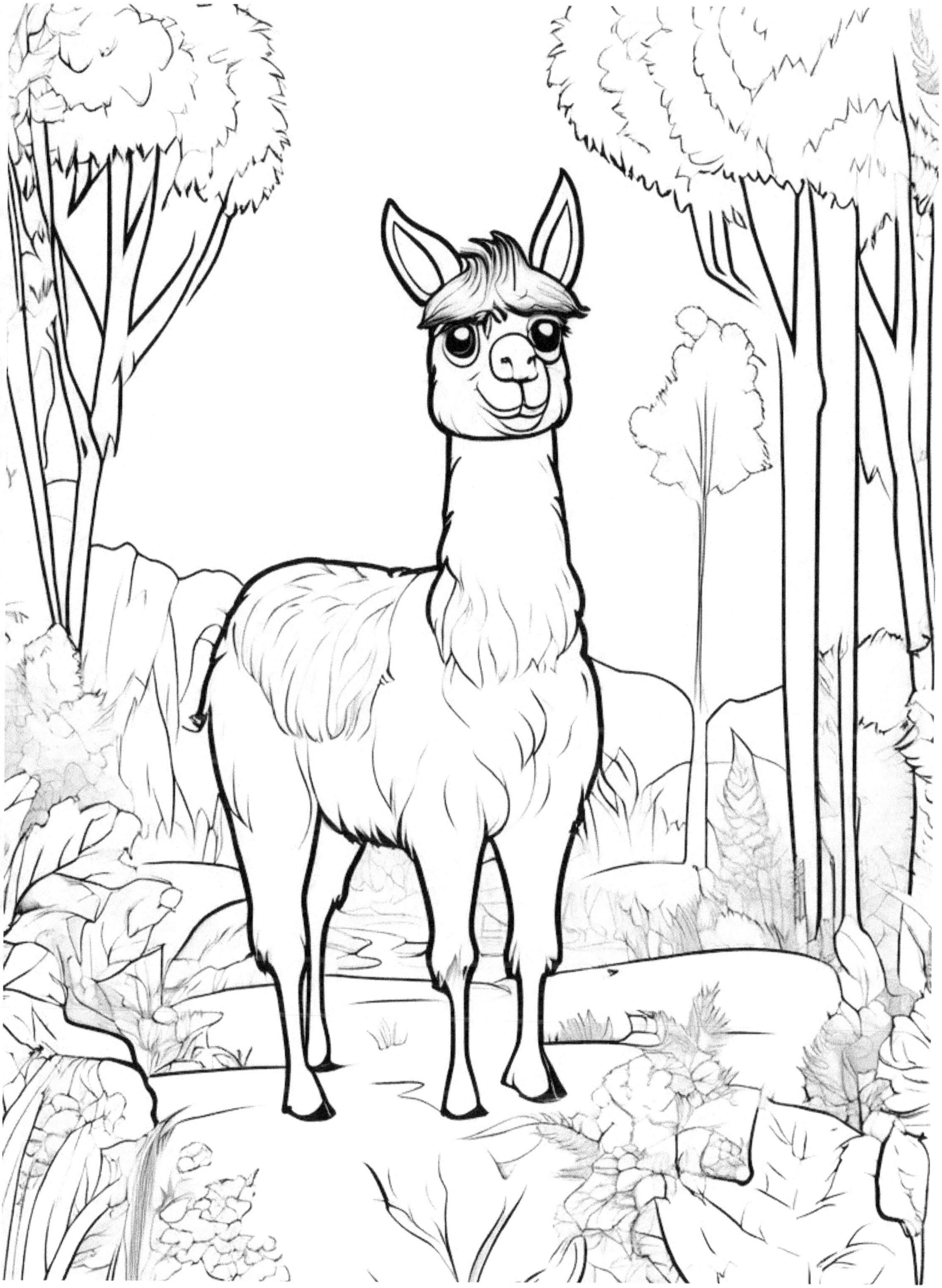

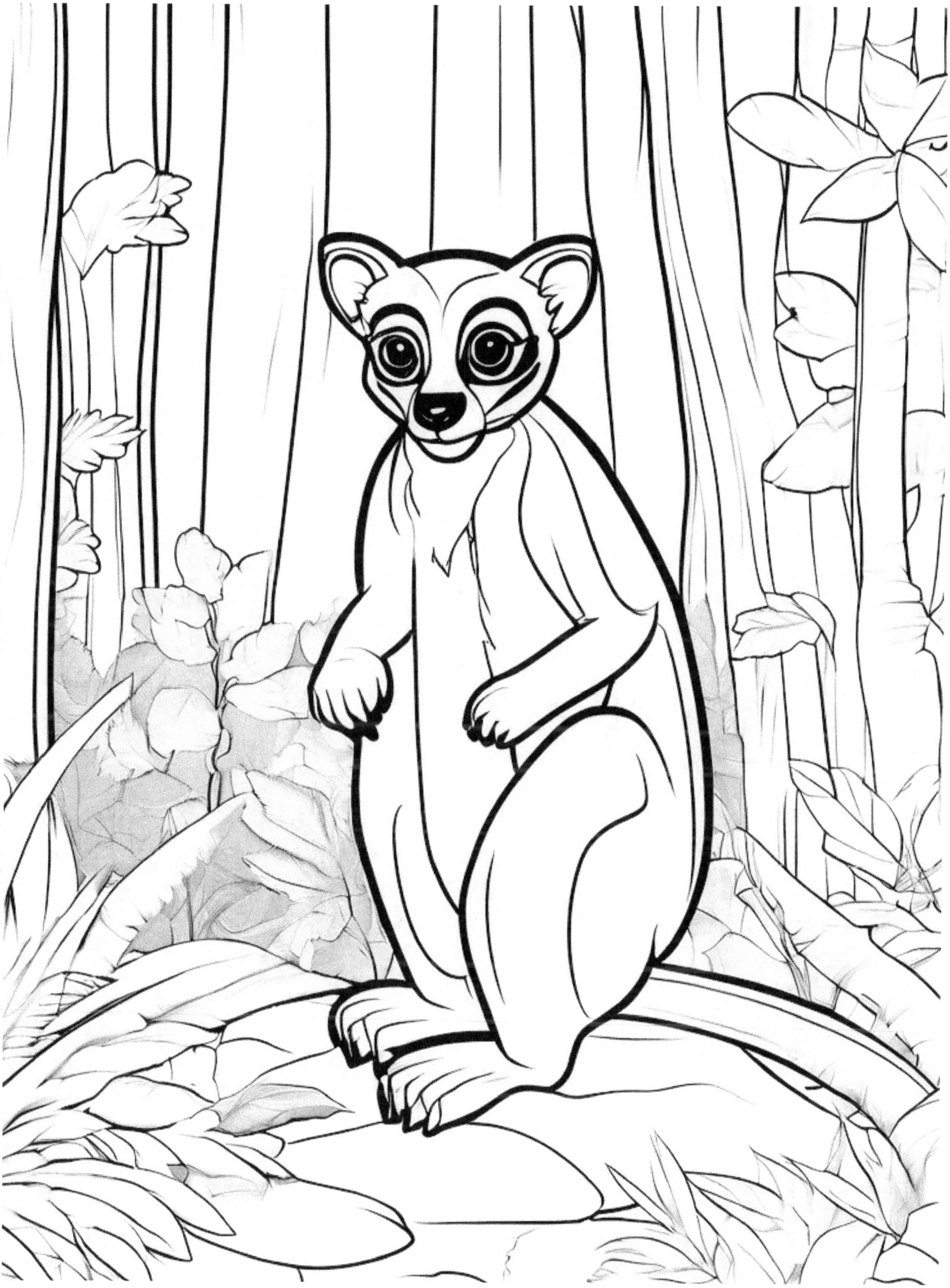

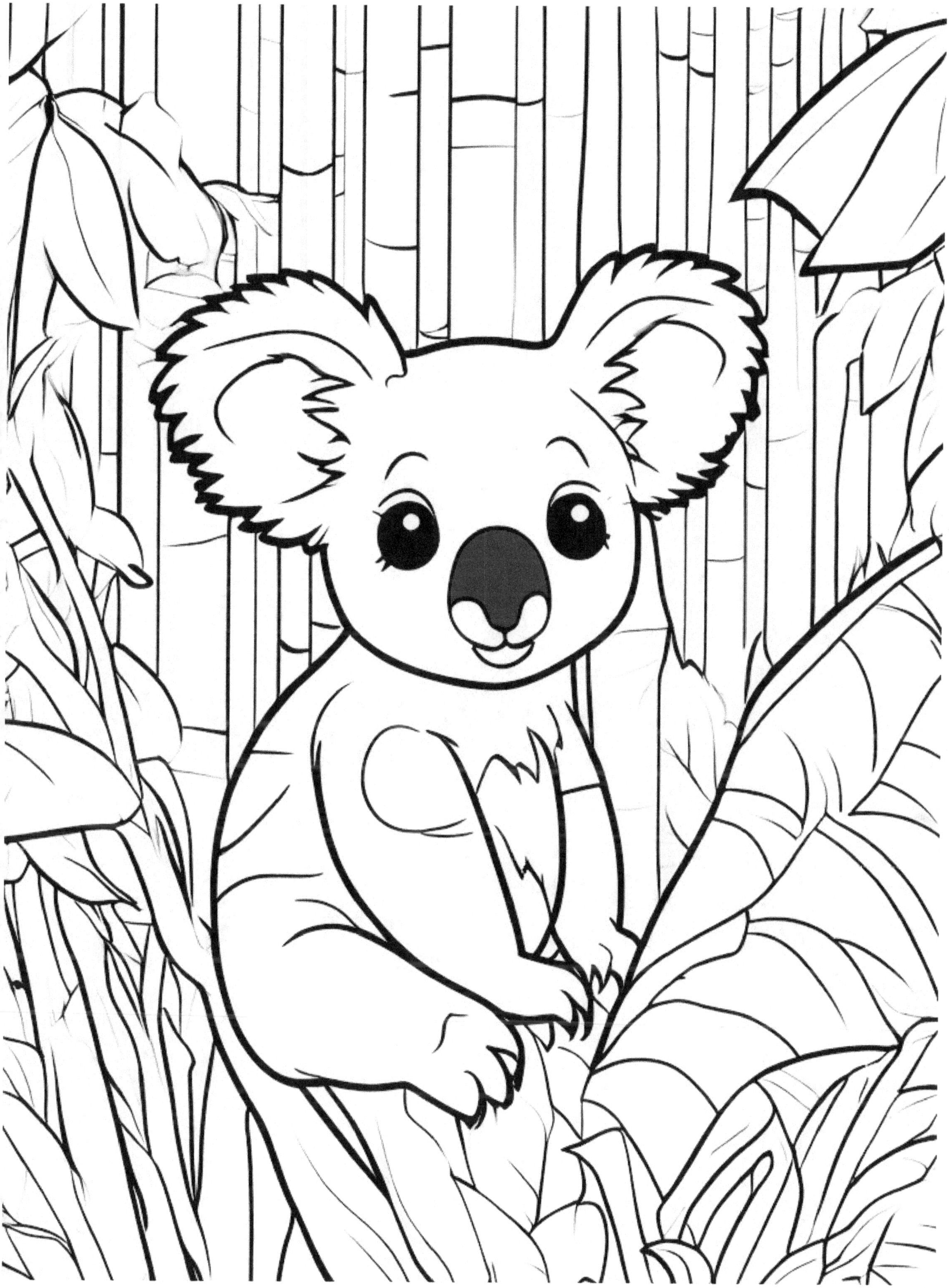

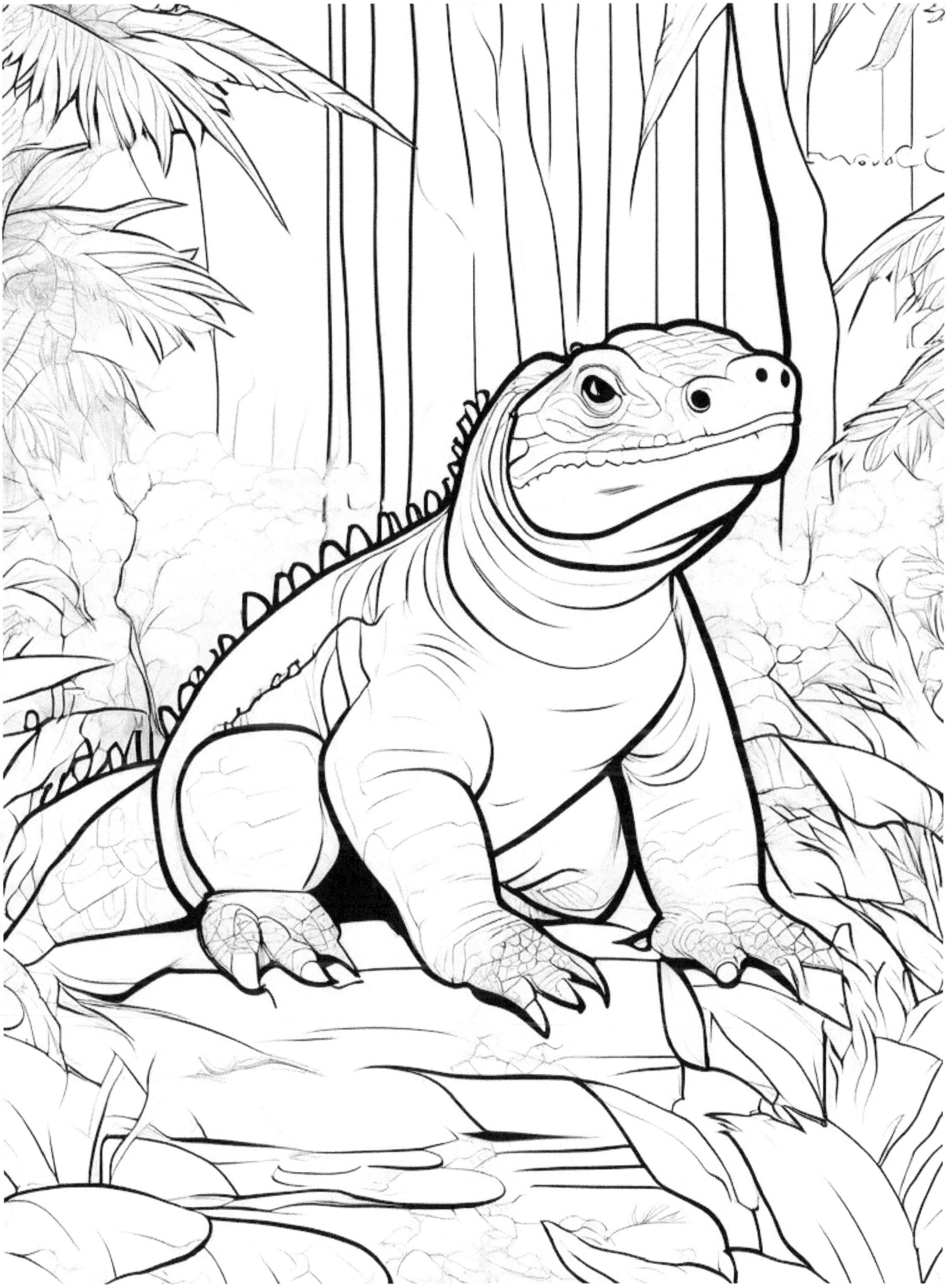

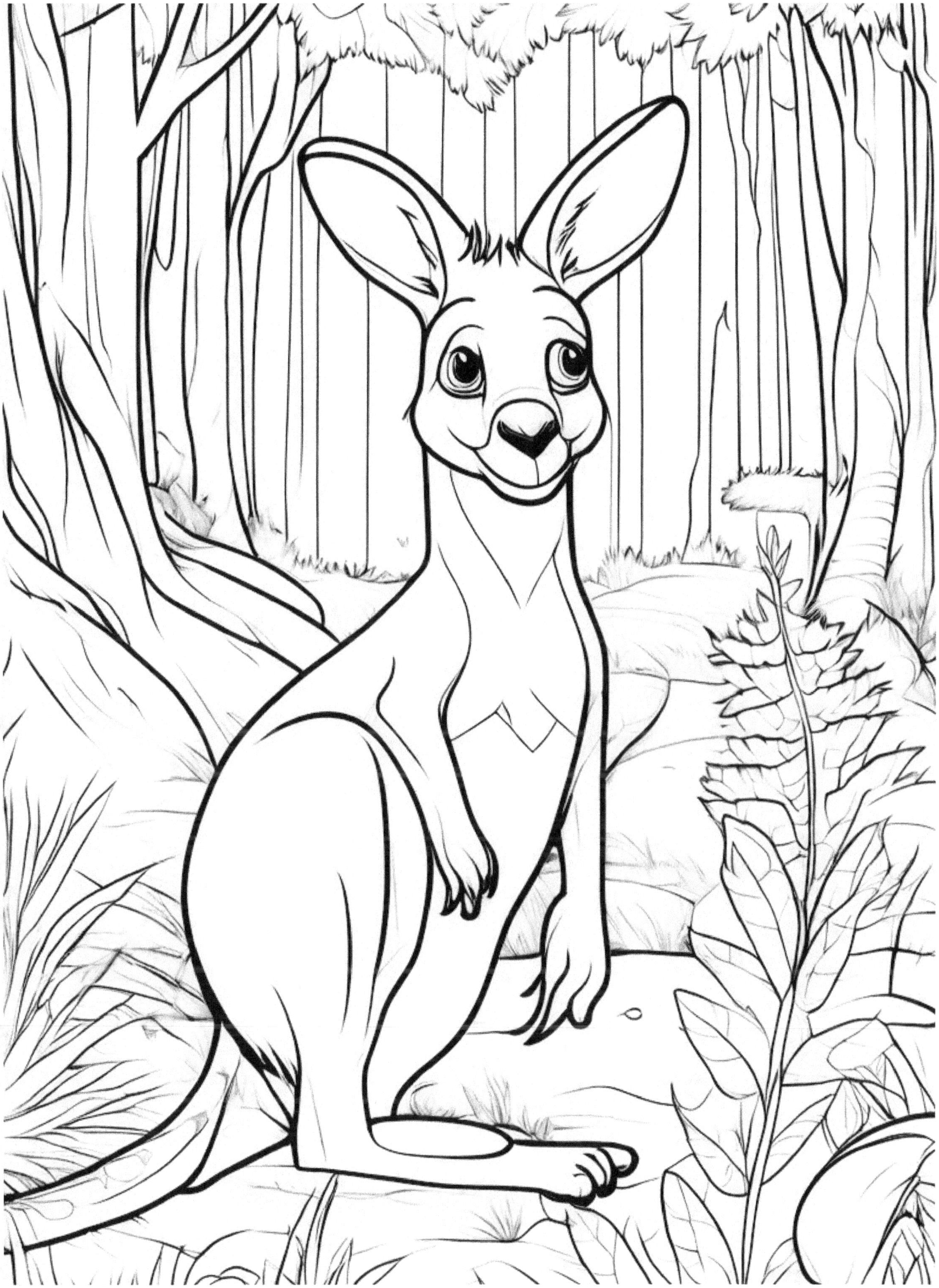

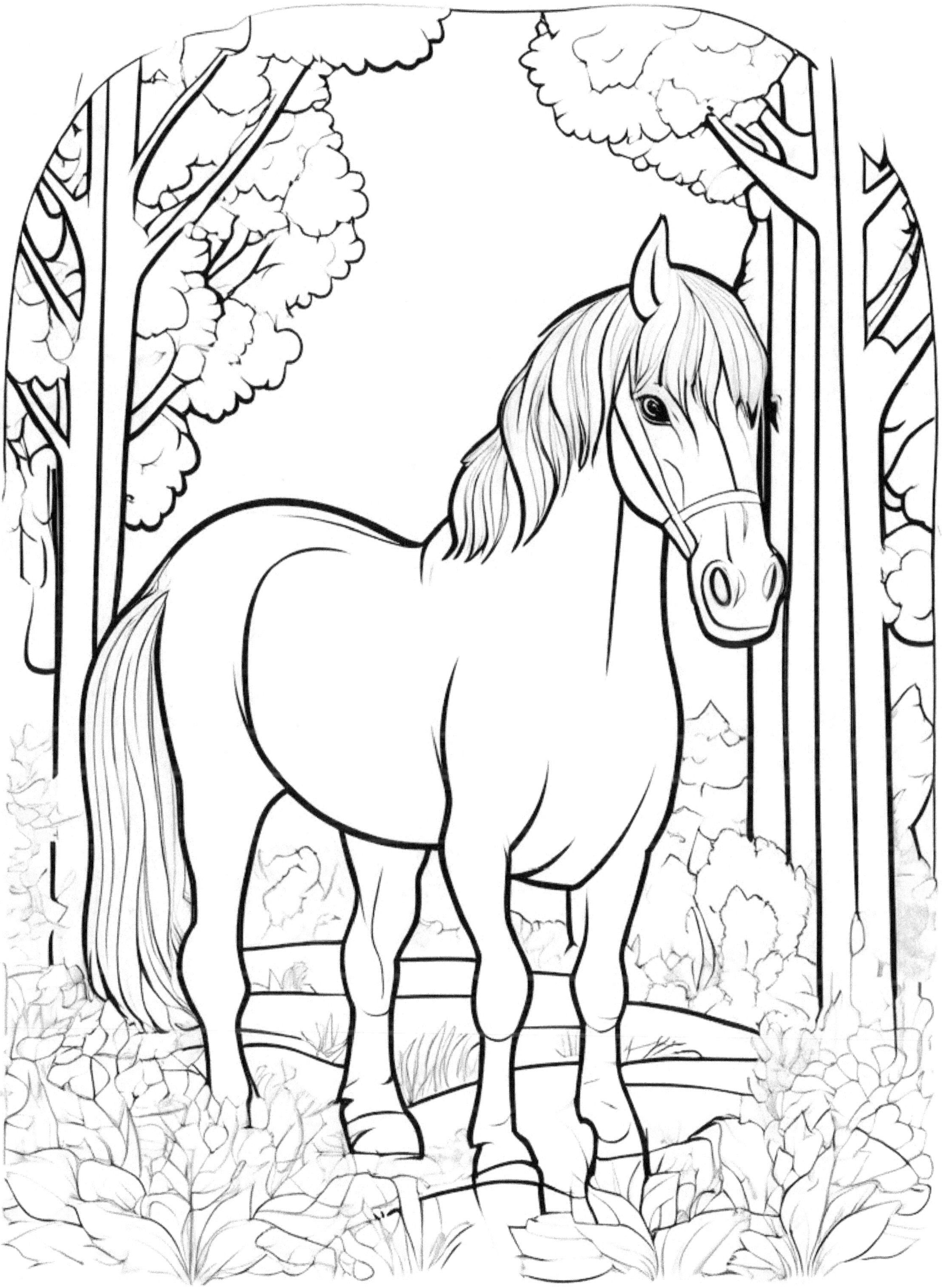

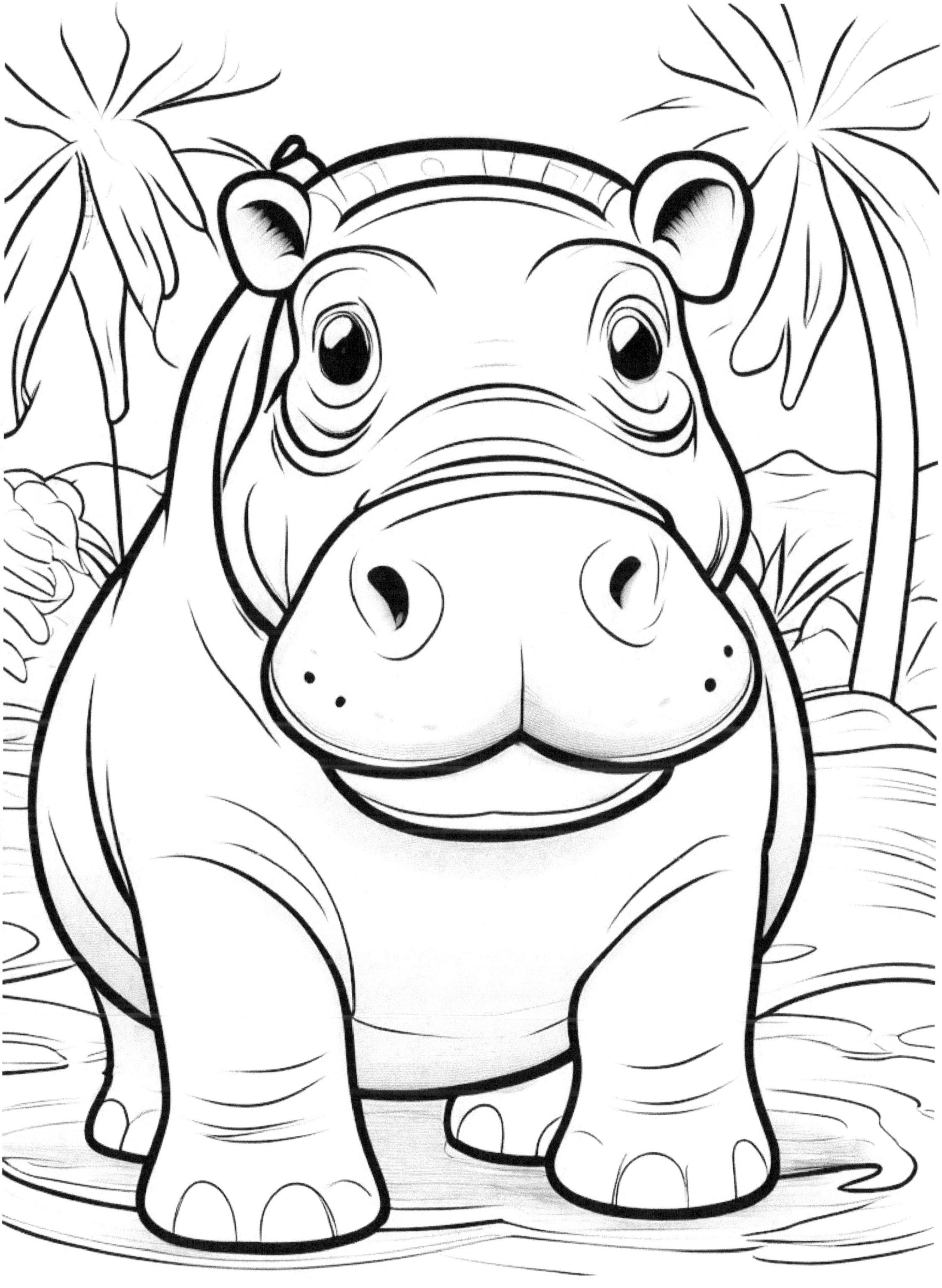

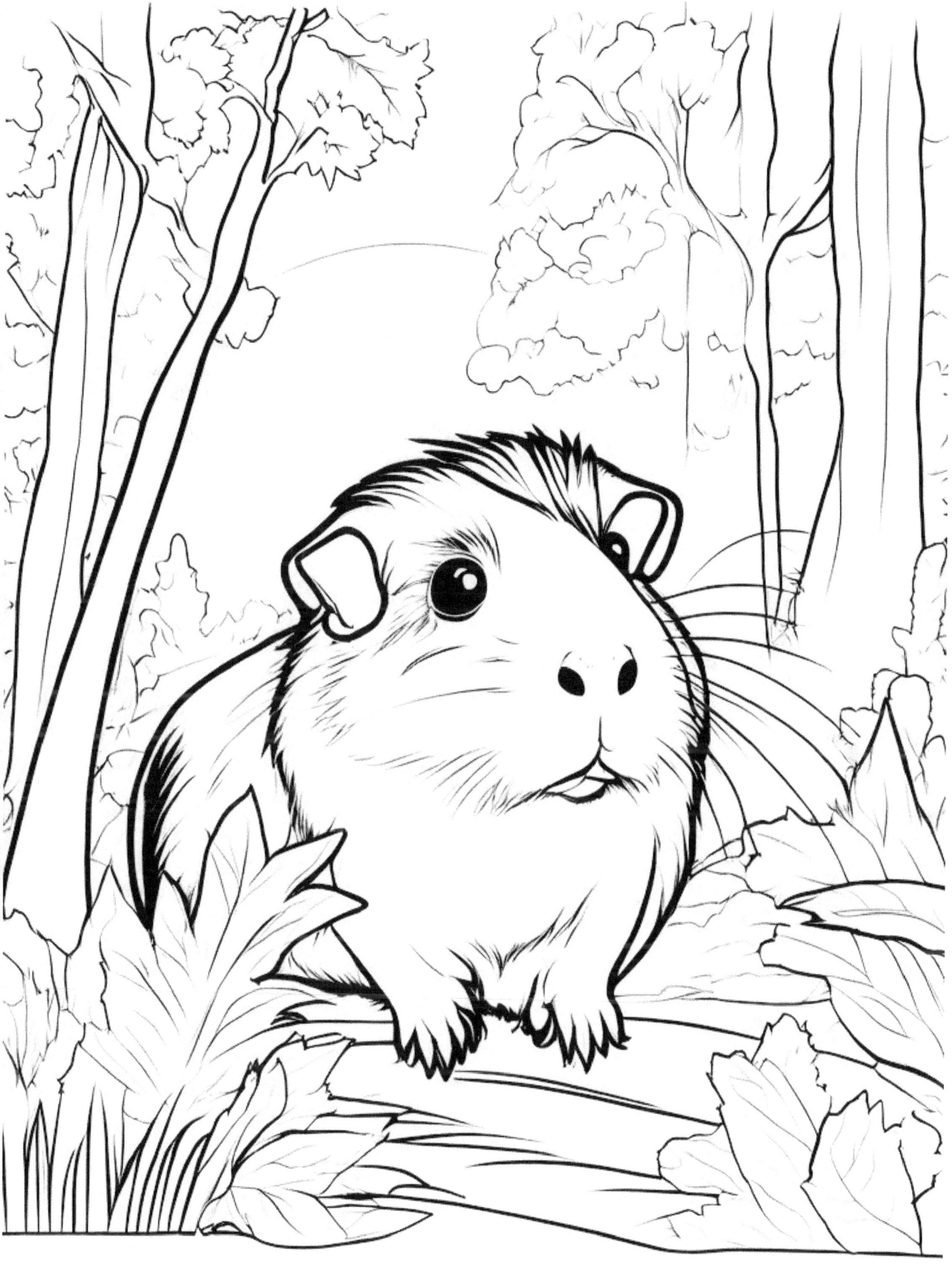

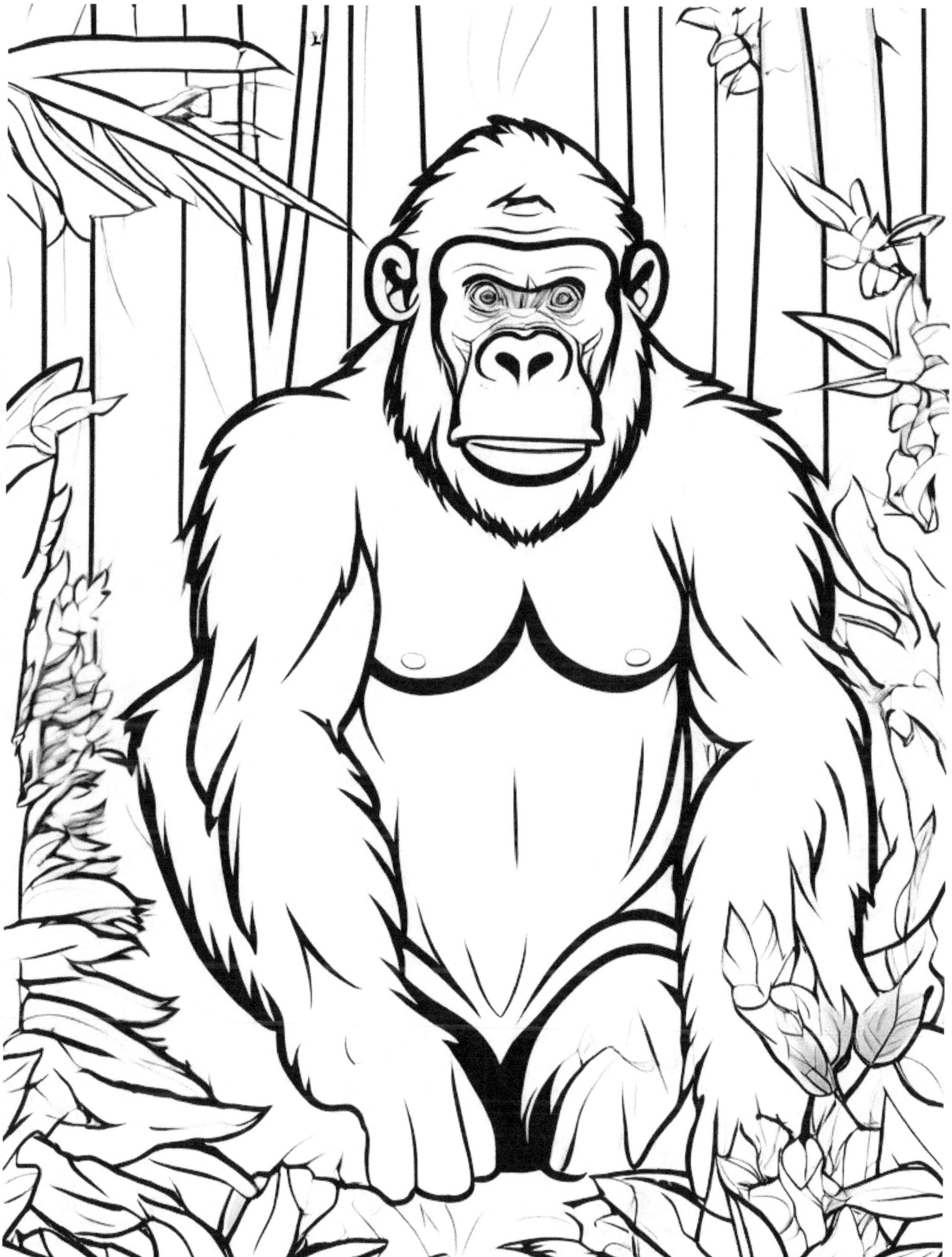

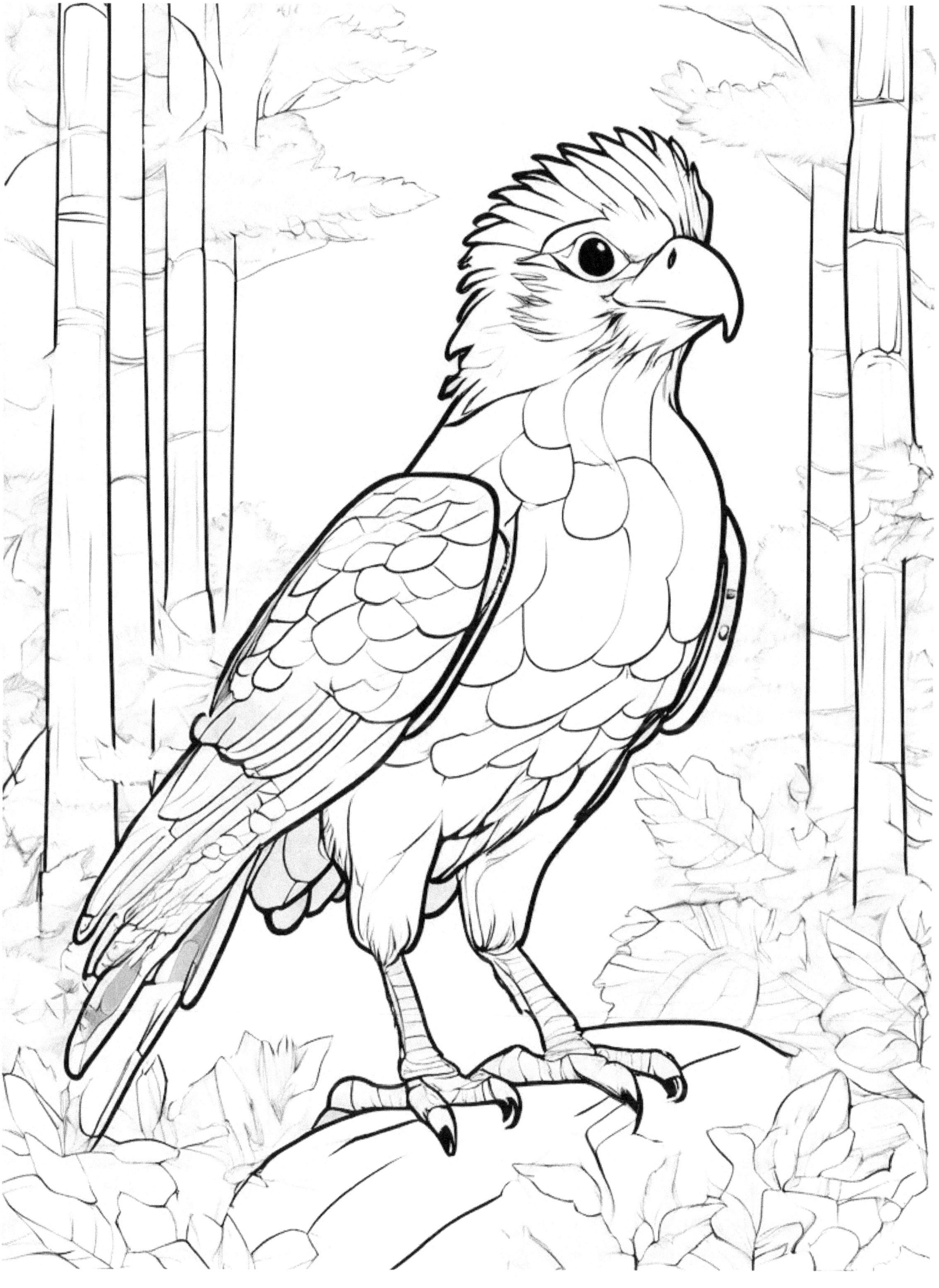

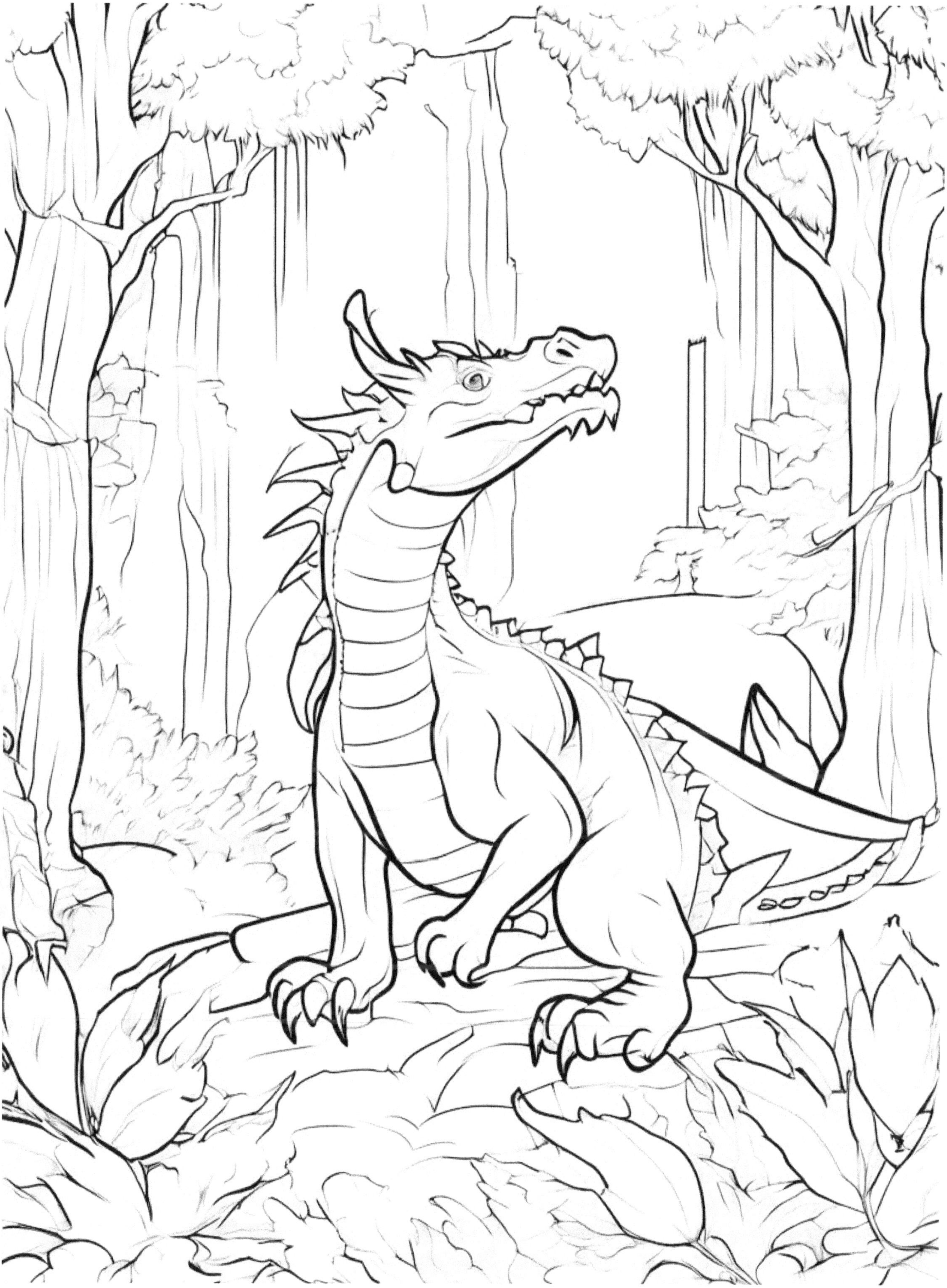

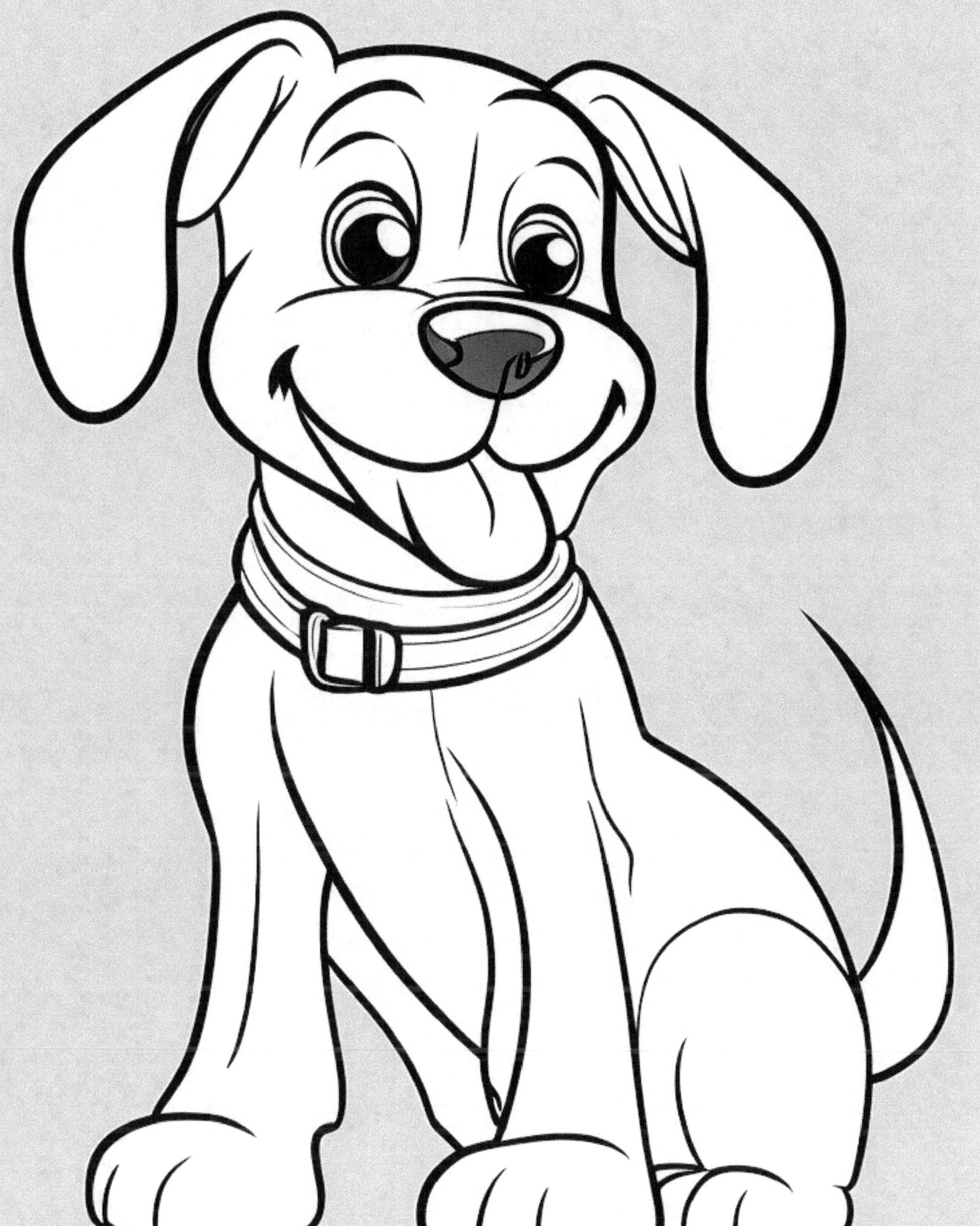

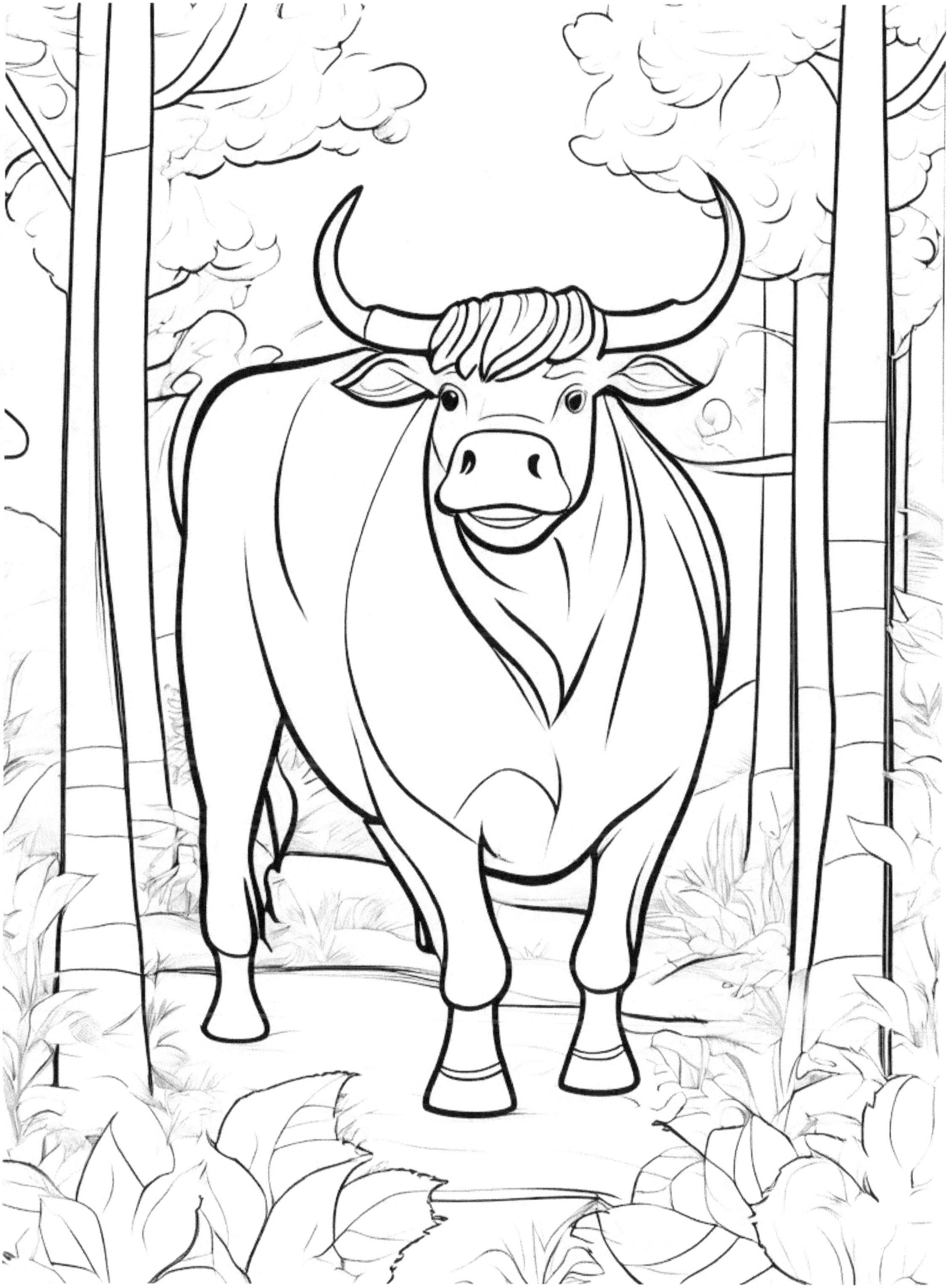

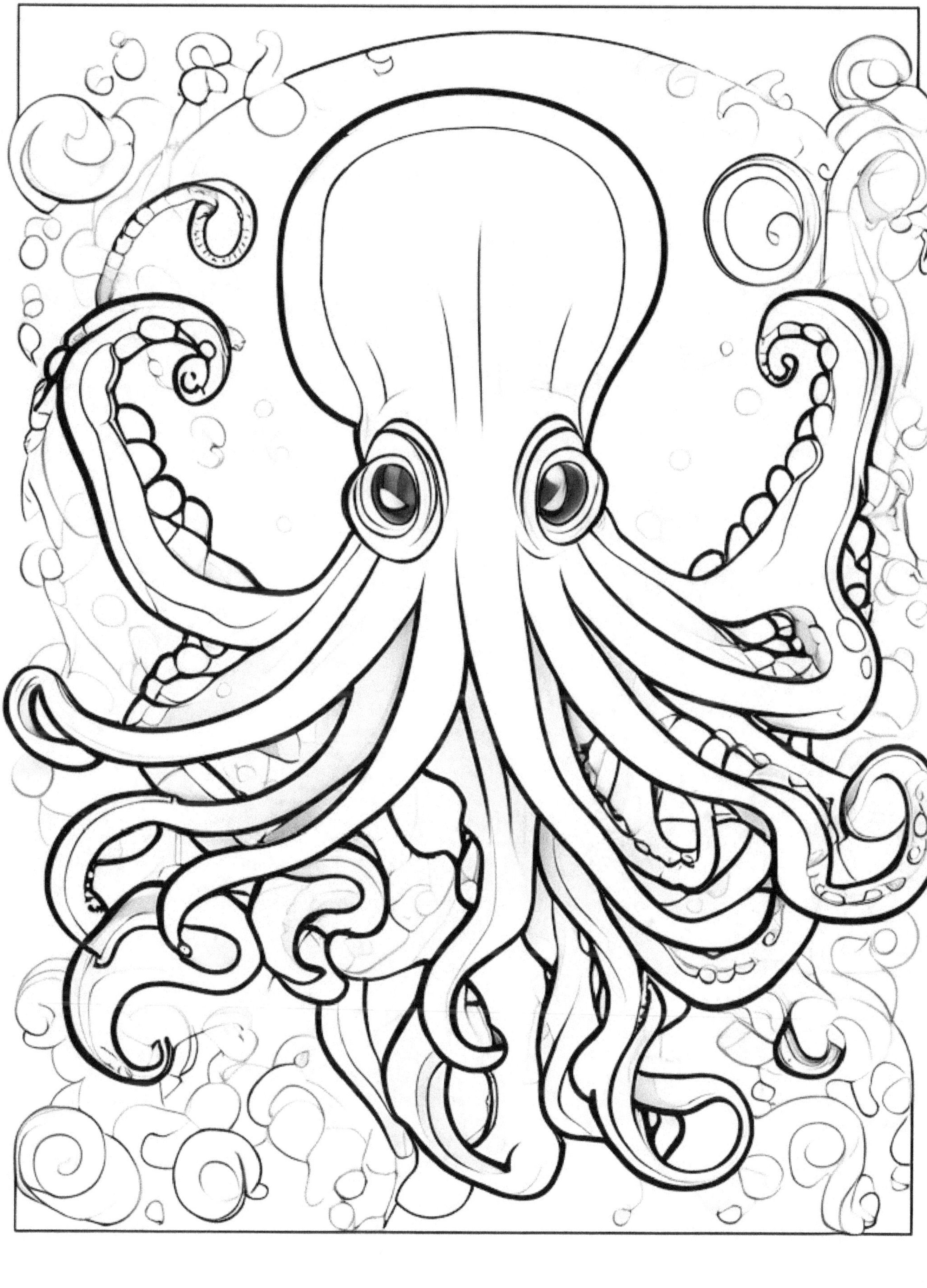

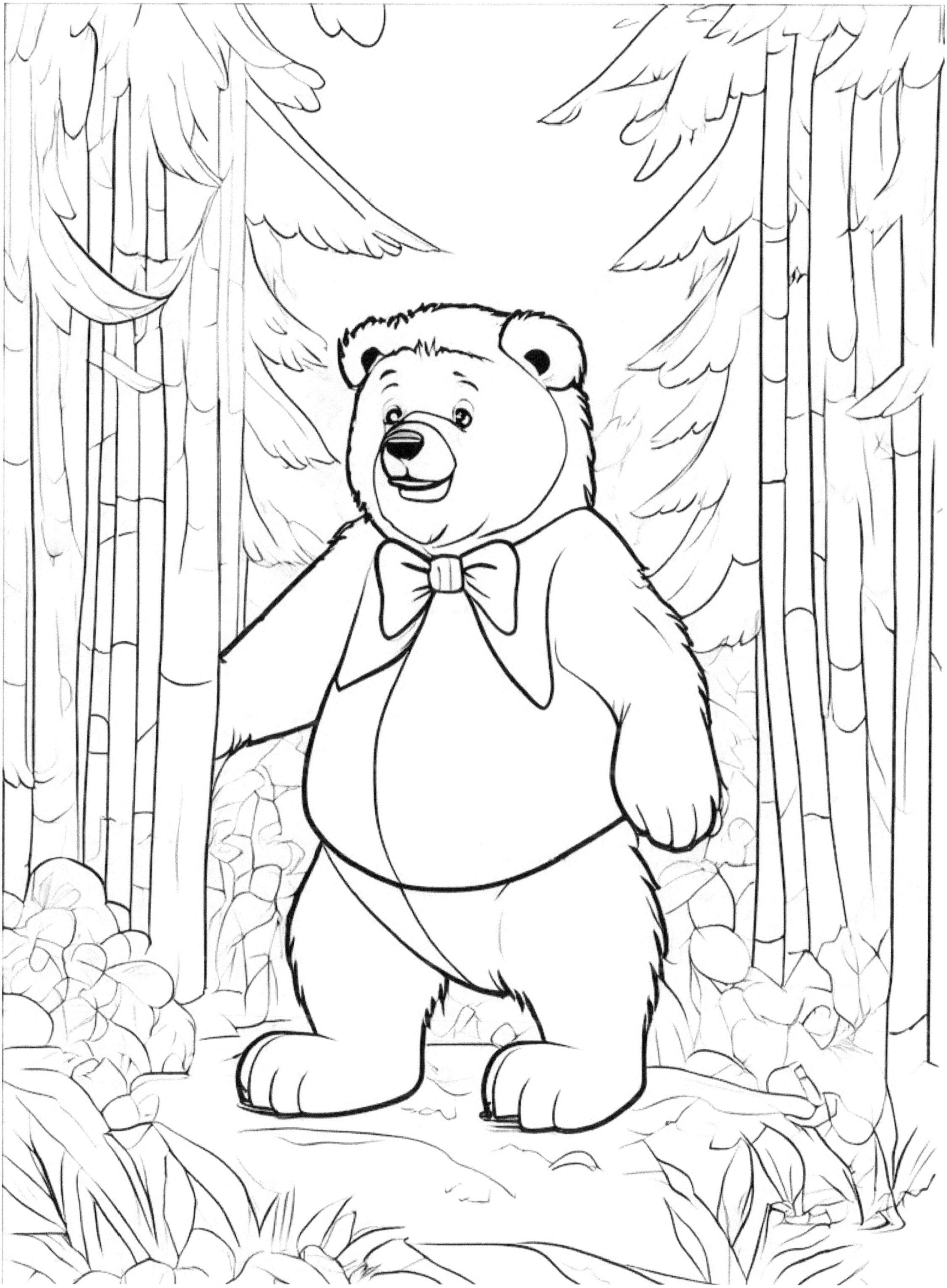

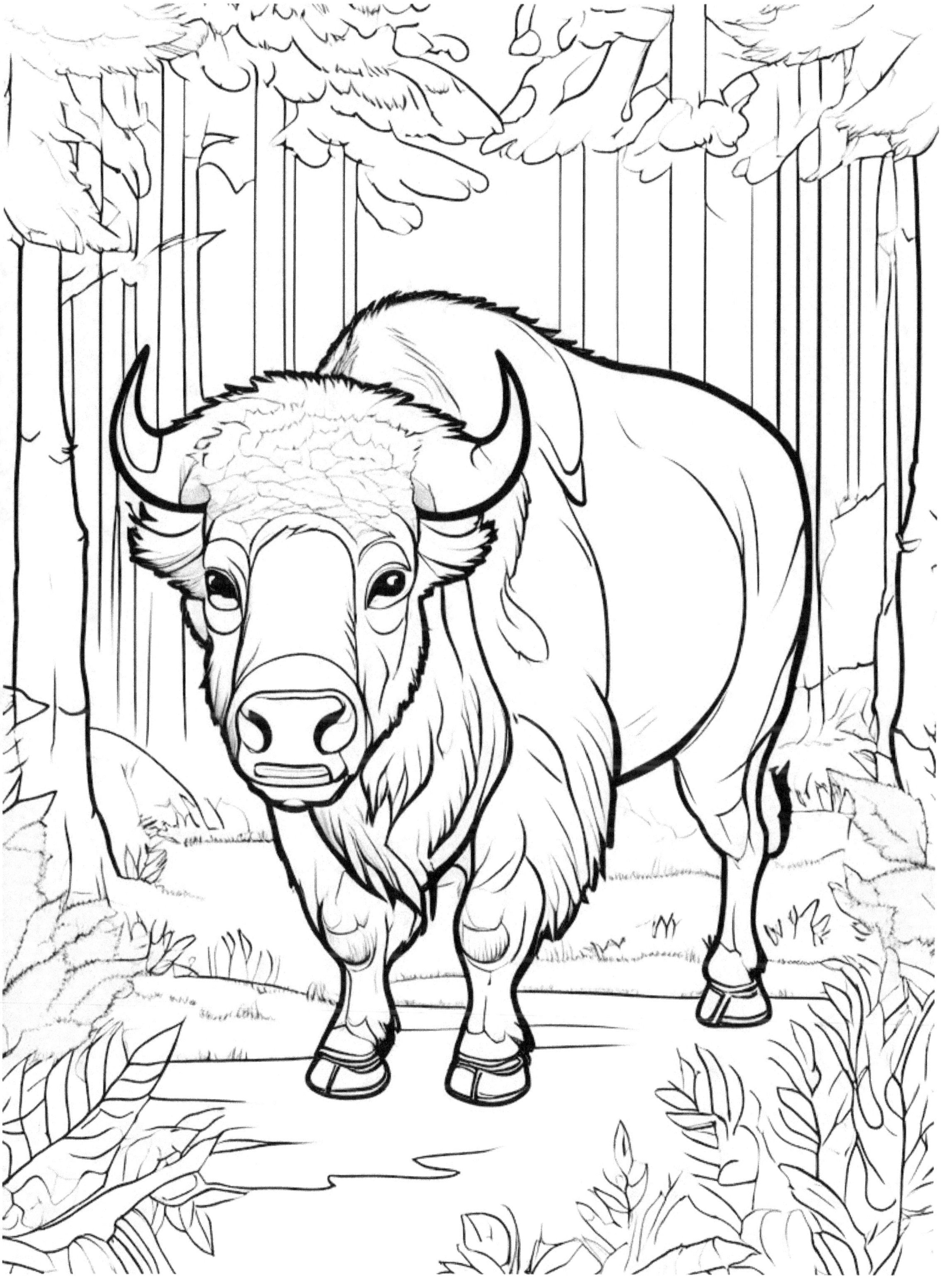

www.ingramcontent.com/pod-product-compliance
Lightning Source LLC
Chambersburg PA
CBHW082355220526
45470CB00008B/2757
* 9 7 9 8 3 2 5 1 0 1 9 7 7 *